IMPRESSIONS
OF A
LAXEY LAD

IMPRESSIONS OF A LAXEY LAD

A Lifetime in
Isle of Man
Publishing and Printing

COLIN BROWN

Published 2012
by
The Manx Experience
Mannin Media Ltd - Media House - Cronkbourne - Isle of Man

*Printed by
Mannin Media Limited - Media House - Cronkbourne - Isle of Man
Telephone 01624 696565*

*To a wonderful wife and
the best family in the world.*

*and to all those colleagues both living and dead
who, between them, managed to make my
working life enjoyable and interesting.*

Thank you.

Introduction

ASK anyone in my family. They will tell you that I have one of the most dreadful memories around! Normally I find it difficult to recall happenings which occured a matter of days previously

Interestingly, in writing this account, I found it relatively easy to recall the early part of my life, whilst the last twenty years or so gave me a great degree of trouble - especially in sorting out the sequence of events. It is said that age affects memory in this manner and perhaps my seventy-odd years is a contributory factor to my normal bad memory.

Whatever the reason or the excuse, it is entirely possible that events may well have occurred either earlier or later than suggested within this account - the one thing of which I am certain is that they did happen!

I also realised, that a broader recall is prompted by describing those instances in your life which do stick in your mind and form major parts of your personal history.

Names, too, have always been a problem for me and so I apologise in advance for any errors or omissions. Many of the characters mentioned have passed away but this does not retract from the impression they created, nor the impact they had, upon my life. I trust that wherever this is so, their descendants will appreciate my memories.

I have been encouraged for a few years to write this account but refrained from doing so basically because I felt that there was insufficient variety in my life to interest a reader.

Now, I really hope that the insistence of my friends is proved to be well-placed and I hope that those who venture to read it will enjoy the story.

Colin Brown
2012

CHAPTER ONE

The Start

W HAT makes you want a career in the printing industry," he enquired, probably expecting a detailed and highly intelligent answer from the rather nervous sixteen-year-old sat opposite.

"Well, I've always wanted to be a printer," was the lame response.

It wasn't, of course, the truth . . .

Harry Norrey, at the time was the Production Manager of the *Isle of Man Times* newspaper, and the reason I was being interviewed in his office was that there was an urgent need for a contribution from me to boost the family income - I needed employment.

My Mum had taken notice of a friend's off the cuff remark that printers fell into the same categories as bakers and funeral directors - that is that their work is always needed! She was also of the view that "all printers are well paid". The friend suggested I should apply for a job to the local newspaper which had recently been acquired by a rich Frenchman and there was a good chance of work.

The rich Frenchman - a certain Henri Leopold Dor - had indeed purchased *Isle of Man Examiner,* then located in premises in Hill Street and, unknown to most, was in the process of also purchasing *Isle of Man Times* - the elder newspaper of the two and based in an equally elderly and substantial building in Athol Street. The *Examiner* was fully staffed, I was advised, but my enquiry had been forwarded to the *Times*.

"You do realise," continued the rather urbane Mr Norrey, "that if you are successful with this application, you will commence an indentured apprenticeship of six years . . ."

He was interrupted by the other gentleman at the desk, "No, Harry, it's recently been renegotiated to five years for a sixteen-year-old. It remains at six years for a fifteen-year-old, but he will be nearly sixteen when he starts and will qualify for the reduced apprenticeship."

Harry Norrey had introduced this chap as Harry Christian, Father of the Chapel.

Such was my ignorance of the industry that I so badly wanted to ask what was the need for a man of religion in a print works. However, it was later patiently explained to me that the Father of the Chapel - usually referred to as the FOC - was the staff's union representative and, at that time, held a responsible position of standing in the company.

Harry Norrey continued his job description.

"The working week is Monday to Friday, 8am to 5.30pm and you are entitled to a lunch break and a mid-morning break, but you will shortly also have to work every other Saturday as the *Examiner* Office publish the *Green Final* on Saturdays and, as they have just bought us out, they will need staff in to cover it. You will be the junior apprentice compositor and will be answerable to Mr Lawson, the composing room foreman. Please remember you will be a compositor, not a printer - printers push buttons!"

It became apparent as the interview progressed that they had decided to offer me the job and, despite the fact that there had been no mention of a wage, when the moment arrived when I was asked if I wished to start in two weeks time, I accepted immediately.

On the bus back to Laxey, I felt excitement mixed with sadness. Sadness, because any hopes of a career in the Royal Navy were well and truly quashed, but excitement, because I was to commence a career in an industry which at that time was well respected and well paid.

Printing and its associated activities were to be my working life and so it began . . .

CHAPTER TWO

Colin Number Two

T HE Jane Crookall Maternity Home in Douglas was, in 1940, a relatively new facility of the Isle of Man Health Services. It was built in pre-war style, with cast iron window frames, but it had nice wide corridors and was comfortable.

There was one waiting room for expectant fathers, but in the main, they were sent packing once they had delivered their spouses to the front door. Fathers were not permitted, in those days, to attend the birth as it was considered that they would only get in the way.

Expectant mothers could choose a bed in the general ward, a semi-private room which catered for two patients or a private room for one. Most mothers opted for a semi-private room and so it was with my Mum when I was about to arrive in this world.

Mum shared a ward with a Mrs Shaw and, as most did in those circumstances, they swiftly became quite friendly. Mrs Shaw, it appears, lived in Hutchinson Square - a nice area just off Broadway - and the two got on like a house on fire.

Mrs Shaw remarked that she had not picked any names for her baby - Mum told her that if it was a boy, she and my Dad had decided he would be called Colin.

"I really like that name," said Mrs Shaw, "would you mind if I used it if mine is a boy?"

"Not at all," said Mum.

I decided to enter the world on 18 November and Colin Number Two arrived four days later on 22nd.

Little did I know how similar and involved our lives would become.

Colin Number One - aged two months.

CHAPTER THREE

Browns of Laxey

ALEXANDER Partington Brown (Alec), my Dad, was part of the family which operated the well-known Brown's Cafe at Dumbell's Terrace in Laxey. The family had entered into the catering business in the period immediately after the First Wold War and, because of its ideal location, on the way to *Lady Isabella* - the Great Laxey Water Wheel - their roast lunches quickly became very popular.

The Brown family was quite large. Dad had two brothers - Kenny and Horace. While Kenny remained in the village, Horace decided at a relatively early age that his future lay in America and he emigrated to Minnesota. Amy, one of dad's sisters, married Tom, a chap from Lancashire, and went to live for the rest of her life in Blackpool. Pat married a Laxey lad, Doug, but they decided to move to Aberystwyth where Doug taught and Pat spent the rest of her life. Lily, Myra and Muriel stayed local, however, and ran the cafe very successfully until Myra's eventual retirement in the mid-1980s.

By 1940 then, Brown's Cafe had been flourishing for many years with the three Brown sisters at the helm.

My Mum, Doris (Dorrie), had arrived in Laxey in 1924 when the Mellor family had taken up residence at South Cape. Mum was still of school age and attended Ramsey Grammar School for a few years after she arrived in the Island.

Mum and Dad met at social occasions in the village - dances and parties were commonplace in the villages around the Island - and they were married at the Registry Office in Douglas in 1935.

A painter and decorator by trade, Dad was very good at his job. Prior to the outbreak of hostilities in 1939, he had been doing well in partnership with Kenny, his brother, and their work was in demand in and around the Laxey area.

Alec Brown - Dad.

Dad responded to the call and in late 1939, volunteered for the Army. His health had never been very good and despite passing the medical for all volunteers, he was invalided out of the forces before he saw any action.

With a desire to serve in some manner, he volunteered for special duties outside of the services and was posted to a factory in Blackpool which was supporting the war effort. He was put in charge of the paint shop.

Amy, Dad's sister, lived in Blackpool and he lodged with her and Tom for many months. Mum and I used to go to see him as often as we could but, in those days, it was quite a long journey especially by steamer to Fleetwood. Occasionally, we flew to Squires Gate airport in those biplanes which had a sloping aisle when you boarded them. It was quite exciting, though.

We lived for a short while in Blackpool where I attended school for my first year.

Eventually, Mum got sick of the arrangement and it was decided that she and I would move to Blackpool to be with Dad.

When the war in Europe ended in 1944, Dad's factory immediately returned to its original function - the supply of hobby-horses and roundabout cars for funfairs. He stayed with the company, however, and ran the paint shop for them.

In the summer of 1945, I was approaching primary school age and Mum and Dad enrolled me in a school in Blackpool which, although I was not yet five, agreed to take me in the September.

I spent an enjoyable first school year in Blackpool and then we all

Grandad Tom Mellor with Mum and me in the garden at "Briardale", South Cape, Laxey. "Ruggy", the family black labrador is featured on the right.

"Ruggy" made this one as well with Auntie Ethel, Nana, Grandad and Mum enjoying the sun at "Briardale".

moved back to Laxey - to my Nana's home at South Cape where she lived with my Auntie Ethel.

It was a sad time. My Grandad, Tom Mellor, who had retired from a career in the Royal Navy as a Chief Petty Officer, suddenly died at the relatively young age of sixty-six. Although I was too young to get to know him really well, he was a portly, generous man who worshipped my Nana. He served throughout the First World War and had a multitude of stories to tell of his experiences around the world.

My Nana's family were Irish and came from Tubbacurry, County Sligo. She and Grandad met during some shore leave he had wangled and, after a brief courtship, they were married in Tubbercurry. Auntie Ethel was born there and shortly afterwards, to suit Grandad's work in the Navy, the family moved to Plymouth where Mum was born.

Following his retirement from the service, Grandad and Nana were appointed wardens of a children's home in Edinburgh with naval connections. They spent many happy years there before relocating to Liverpool where they ran a greengrocery store, apparently, not with a great deal of success!

Grandad had been to the Island previously and liked the place - he decided that the Island would be their final residence and they moved in 1924. He was highly respected within the service and when it became obvious that war was a possibility for the second time, he was appointed RN recruiting officer for the Isle of Man.

I think it may well have been Grandad's passing, coupled with the draw of the Island, which affects most Manx-born people, that brought my Dad back to Laxey. He began work once again as a painter and decorator and quickly established a tidy clientele.

THE headmaster of Laxey Primary School was Mr Killip. He was a kindly man and made me very welcome when I attended for the first time. Apparently,

Auntie Myra along with her sisters, successfully ran Brown's Cafe at Ham and Egg Terrace Laxey for many years. Here she is pictured outside the cafe with her two nephews - my cousin, Nornan and myself.

Laxey Harbourmaster, Edwin Cregeen, later to feature heavily in my life, leads a group of 'fishermen' onto the playing field at Glen Road, for the Manx Wedding. Some of the participating children, excited at the forthcoming event, bring up the rear.

(Left) My Uncle Kenny with his 'wife', for the purposes of the Manx Wedding, Irene Gelling, promenade after the ceremony as part of the procession.

he was of the view that the year I had completed at Blackpool meant that I should miss the beginners' year and I should start in Miss Richards' class. 'Fanny', as she was widely known, was quite a character by all accounts. She was feared by all of her pupils, not because she was overly severe, but unfortunately she possessed a very deep voice and, when she gave an instruction, it had a booming effect which scared the daylights out of most children.

Not long after my arrival at the school, Fanny presented me with a planted shrub in its pot.

"Take it to the Hall please, Colin, and don't fall it," she boomed.

Now my education up to that time had not been extensive, to say the least, but I knew she was wrong. I realised later on in life that this phraseology was common in Manx conversation and is still often heard today.

I haven't a clue where the courage came from but I quickly replied, "Yes, Miss Richards, I won't drop it."

She stared at me for quite a while. "Thank you," she said.

It was an enjoyable time at Laxey School. We had nice grounds to the school which meant that we could spend quite a large amount of time outdoors playing sports and PE.

The school took part in a 'Manx Wedding' which was organised for the village as a whole. The preparations within the school went on for weeks beforehand and on the day we took part in the dancing and in the procession through the village. The actual 'wedding' took place in the Glen Road football field which was relatively adjacent to the school. It was a lovely day with lots of music from brass bands and small music groups and the village really came together to ensure the event's success.

Peter Creer lived next door to us at South Cape. We became best mates and used to walk together to and from school. Francis Lowey lived on Old Laxey Hill and he, too, was part of my circle in early life.

CHAPTER FOUR

"Ainslie"

BY 1947, family life in Laxey was enjoyable and my Mum added to it when she announced during that summer that I was to have a brother. He was born on Christmas Eve 1947 and his arrival at Christmas ensured that he would be called Nicholas.

Mum always tried very hard to keep Nick's birthday on Christmas Eve and his associated birthday presents completely separate from the Christmas presents the following day. I'm not so sure she was always successful, and I have a feeling that Nick always suffered because of the unfortunate timing of his birth. I know the materialism of presents should not be the major factor in these celebrations, but to a child, the fact is that they definitely are important.

Mum and Dad had been keen to move to their own home and Nick's arrival added to that. Eventually they acquired a property on the main road to Ramsey close to Minorca crossroads.

"Ainslie" was a pre-war three-bedroomed semi with a nice long front garden and a small back plot set down to vegetables. The front gate opened directly onto the main road and was quite dangerous. I well recall the firm instructions to "be very careful when you go out the front way." There was also a lovely front lounge which, as it was on the northern side of the Laxey valley, benefitted from afternoon sunshine.

Bill Edwards, the well-known local photographer lived next door and

Nick's arrival on Christmas Eve 1947, brought about a move to the Ramsey Road.

immediately made us very welcome. Bill was always happy to explain his skills to anyone who was prepared to listen and I spent quite a few hours in the darkroom he had set up in his home. He showed me some of the techniques of his trade but I'm afraid none of them remained with me and to this day, if a camera isn't automatic, I'm a useless photographer!

Living at "Ainslie" was closer to school and meant that I could get home faster when the afternoon bell went.

By this time I had my own bicycle and spent many hours cycling around the village. I seemed to have been surrounded by namesakes in my young life and one of the sons of our neighbours, Mr and Mrs Towers, was also called Colin. He was a very keen amateur cyclist and was a member of one of the Isle of Man cycling clubs. On one afternoon run with the club, Colin was involved in a horrific accident near Ramsey in which he nearly lost his life. In those days, helmets were not part of the normal cycling apparatus. Colin spent many months in hospital as a result and the incident brought home the dangers of the sport. I was very careful on my bike for a long time afterwards!

As 1950 approached, I was invited to sit the entrance examination for bursary attendance at King William's College. 'King Bill's', as it was commonly called, was highly recognised as the premier educational establishment in the Isle of Man and, if you were an ex-pupil of 'King Bill's', your professional career was greatly enhanced.

The problem for me was that I didn't want to be a boarder and to travel the fourteen miles each way every day was a bit much. Privately, I didn't like the thought of having to make new friends and that they would "all be too stuck up anyway." The convincing argument for me was that I would probably not be entering the professions anyway - a trade was the most likely career for me.

So, although I sat the exam to satisfy Laxey School, I did it with very little enthusiasm and wasn't the least bit surprised when I was notified of a failure - in fact, I was rather pleased!

Ballakermeen Secondary School presented a much better option for me. Most of my mates would be going there, although some did go to Ramsey Grammar because, as pupils in Laxey, we were located midway between both schools, and had the option of either.

CHAPTER FIVE

"Balla and the Back Entrance"

I JOINED Form 1S at "Balla" in September 1950. I was two months short of my eleventh birthday and immediately walked into a completely different educational environment.

The difference between Laxey Primary and Ballakermeen Junior school was startling. All the "childishness" of the primary school had disappeared. You knew you were at Ballakermeen to be educated and you'd better believe it! Three lessons each morning and three each afternoon: Maths (Algebra and Geometry) - Chemistry, Geography, History, Physics, English, French, Art, and the PE sessions and sports. Swimming was in the in-school baths with the walkthrough footpaths to ensure there was no epidemic of verrucas!

Compared to the modern day, discipline was strict - form masters still wore their gowns which invariably concealed a cane and they were not averse to using it when required. Pieces of blackboard chalk occasionally flew around the classroom sometimes with deadly accuracy, and the blackboard duster or the edge of the wooden ruler often found the back of the hand of some irreverent pupil.

One well-known teacher favoured a slipper - a large one which must have been a size 14 at least. He often applied this to young arses, the owners of which had been particularly obstreperous. He carried the nickname "Slipper" Smith and was known by that name long after his retirement.

In later life "Slipper" became a very keen golfer and could often be seen at Peel Golf Club. His ability to administer corrective action with the slipper, however, remained with him and many of his colleagues used to use his nickname.

The sports facilities at Ballakermeen were good with a large playing field in front of the school and the excellent swimming bath which was quite a major step forward for educational establishments at the time. I clearly remember a swimming instructor who took a great delight in pushing those pupils who were not too keen on swimming into the shallow end. He took the view that once you are wet you might as well join in. It's rather doubtful that he would get away with it in the present days of "elf 'n safety"!

The playing field was used for football and cricket and cross-country running was a popular event for the sports masters. I loved it all, less so the running as I was always a bit of a lazy sod.

I worked hard to get in the first form football team and managed it for two matches, but although I thoroughly enjoyed it, I could never have been much good at cricket.

We were also playing a lot of football at home. For the purpose of forming a "Junior League" the village was divided into four zones and youngsters living in each zone played for their team. The zones played one another regularly, often with only six or seven in the team, and sometimes in ludicrous locations.

I remember playing for "South Cape and Fairy Cottage" against "The Village and Baldhoon" and the match was played at a place called The Fifty - about two miles up Baldhoon Hill towards the mountains. The walk up the hill from the village tired all the lads out before the match was played and there weren't too many spectators, either! "Glen Road and Minorca" was another of the village's teams.

Most of the matches, however, were played at Glen Road pitch where the village senior team played, but we had to be careful as the club officials were always keen to keep the pitch in a reasonable condition. It meant that we often were forced to play across the pitch from touchline to touchline instead of using the full length in order not to use the goal areas.

THE tourist business in the early 1950s was very good. The country was just beginning to pick itself up after the war and people were keen to get a holiday away from the UK mainland and the Isle of Man was the choice of many. Thousands used to reach the Island by steamer from Ardrossan during the Glasgow Fair fortnight in July and the workers in the cotton mills of Lancashire and Yorkshire used to have their fortnight's annual holiday just prior to the Scottish invasion.

Television, though still in its relative infancy, was becoming more widespread and professional wrestling was broadcast every Saturday afternoon fronted by Kent Walton.

As ever, there must have been a few entrepreneurs around at the time as someone had the bright idea of bringing the same wrestlers to the Isle of Man as a seasonal attraction and the "arena" area at Laxey Glen Gardens were chosen as the perfect venue. The arena consisted of a square of four or five concrete levels built so as to allow each level to be higher than the level in front and to afford a view of the centre.

The wrestling ring - the real McCoy by the way - was erected in the centre and was covered with a canopy which meant that a shower of rain was insufficient to halt the proceedings.

The events were invariably quite hilarious affairs. Everyone knew that a degree of showmanship was part of the proceedings and that very few of the wrestling bouts consisted of true wrestling. There were always the "bad" guys and the "good" guys.

It meant that TV names such as Bert Royal, Kendo Nagasaki and Jumping Jim Hussey could be seen most weeks at Laxey. The events quickly became very popular and sometimes were on three times a week. Attendances became so good that on most occasions, motor coaches which had brought the tourists to the village from Douglas were parked nose-to-tail along the main Douglas-Laxey road, the main Ramsey-Laxey road and along a major portion of Mines Road.

There was a constant demand for photographs and autographs of the wrestling "stars". The good guys were always beseiged when they finished their bout - the "baddies" were treated with some care!

The events were full of excitement for us kids who had watched Kent Walton's shows regularly and we just had to get in to see them live. It was quite expensive to get in to the shows - the promoters must have made a lot of money out of them - and it was far above our meagre means.

So we had to get in another way and, eventually, the problem was simply solved . . . we "broke in"!

In those days, Laxey Glen Gardens were privately owned and cared for and there was a small charge to get in at the main gate just to see the gardens themselves. However, if you were prepared to walk through some fields and some quite heavy undergrowth, climb over the old water supply system to the Flour Mill and walk down the bank, you could actually get in for nothing - our entrance to the wrestling - and we used it for many years!

We had to be careful, of course, and make sure we were not accosted by the reputed "armed guards who were patrolling the grounds." Utter nonsense, of course, but enough to scare the wits out of us young rascals.

We managed see many wrestling matches and enjoyed every one, however, we always kept a wary eye out for what could be a "plain clothes policeman"!

CHAPTER SIX

Jack the Lad

BY THE time I had progressed to the second year at Ballakermeen, I had joined the 10th Douglas Boy Scouts which were based at Ballakermeen and were run by Jack Gair, who was one of the school's senior masters and was particularly well-known throughout the local scouting world.

Jack was the most enthusiastic man I have ever met. He worked tirelessly for his "lads" as he called us and his enthusiasm was so infectious he never had a problem obtaining support from parents for any Scout effort.

Jack was adept at raising money for the scout troop in any way possible: jumble sales, concerts, sponsored walks, you name it - Jack would take it on. His aim was always to reduce any financial burden on the parents whilst at the same time ensuring that his lads benefitted from all of the advantages and enjoyment provided by scouting. He seemed invincible and was a true leader of both scouts and their parents. The scout uniform itself was quite expensive, so Jack made sure that the contribution from troop funds towards each lad's uniform was sufficient to make it affordable for the parents.

The man had the most fantastic memory and when I met him just a few years ago, despite his advancing years - he was in his early 90s - and his acute deafness, he immediately recognised me and we were able to enjoy a good chat! Unfortunately he passed away in 2010.

The scout troop met every week in the winter. We learned many country crafts and each scout worked hard for his badges which were awarded at each efficiency level.

There were regular camps to Glen Wyllin and to Mull-ny-Carty when the outdoor training was tested to the full. However, the highlight of the scouting year was always the summer camp. Jack Gair helped many young lads, including myself, to make their first foray abroad and, for some, their first trip away from the Island.

I was fortunate to go to Ireland twice with the scouts - to camp at Annamoe in County Wicklow - and to visit Denmark and France to attend

Jack Gair took 10th Douglas scout troop to Annamoe in County Wicklow, Ireland on two separate occasions for the summer camp - I was fortunate to be included each time and thoroughly enjoyed the experience.

jamborees in each country. Normally there were around twenty scouts and three or four scout masters, including Jack, accompanying the group. Security was strict but, in fairness, there was never any desire by the scouts to bend the rules especially whilst in transit.

There were a couple of amusing episodeswhich I well recall.

Firstly, the occasion in Annamoe when the singing around the camp-fire became rather boisterous mainly due to the few bottles of "brown stuff" which had been "given" by the local shopkeeper to the "lads camping up the road"! We were banned from leaving the campsite the following day!

Then there was the jamboree in Denmark which was held in Esbjerg, a southern coastal city. We travelled to Esbjerg by overnight ferry from Harwich and were met on the quayside by the local Danish scout troop. In his normal attempt to conserve costs to his lads, Jack had arranged for each Manx scout to board with a Danish scout's family for a week prior to the jamboree.

Introductions were made and we each disappeared with our allotted Danish families. Mine turned out to be a lovely family of five - Mum, Dad, son, daughter and Grandma - who resided in what appeared to be quite an expensive area of the city.

After a good night's sleep recovering from the sleep lost on the

My scout uniform may differ somewhat to today's more modern attire, but the principles of scouting remain and they always provide a good grounding for future life.

ferry, breakfast was served to the family. I noticed some bread, fruit, meats and what appeared to be a large bowl of hot porridge which was in the centre of the table. I love porridge and accepted an invitation to have some and, feeling rather hungry, dug in.

It was not porridge! The nearest I can describe it is that it was buttermilk - the side product of butter making and in those days a popular item used for baking - which had been thickened and heated.

It was very, very sour and although I tried hard not to show it, it was clear that the family were amused by my reaction to it. The family proceeded to eat it by dipping the rather delicious bread into it and adding some of the fruit. I'm afraid that, hungry as I was, I could not stomach the liquid and I had to make do with some of the meat and fruit.

Nevertheless, the remainder of the stay with my new Danish family was exceptional. They made me very welcome and asked many questions about the Isle of Man. I made a firm friend of Eidur, the scout, and we were able to meet up a couple of times at the jamboree the following week.

The scouts brought forth new friends - Geoff Rome, whom I had known for many years in Laxey, was also a member of 10th Douglas and he became my big buddy - Peter Clague, lived in Douglas but through his regular attendance at scouts, he too became a firm friend.

The scouts became so popular that Jack Gair had to form three separate troops - the original Scouts, a troop of Sea Scouts and a troop of Air Scouts. Terry Corteen who had joined the Sea Scouts, also became one of our friends and the gang prospered.

PETER, Geoff and I loved sport and football in particular. Peter played at the time for a junior Douglas team and Geoff and I were part of the junior squad at Laxey. But we all supported the senior team which, in the case of Laxey, was quite successful at the time. We watched many a closely fought match from the "broogh" - the grass bank on the north side of the pitch at Glen Road, and a natural grandstand. I well recall a couple of Laxey wins over Peel - the in-form team of the day - in league matches when, on both occasions, tempers became rather frayed and the referee was somewhat busy.

Doug Baird, who worked as a linotype operator in the newspaper offices of *Isle of Man Times* and who later became goalkeeper for the Isle of Man First XI, John Gordon (centre half) and his brother Charlie (centre forward and also an Island international), Maurice Faragher (half back), Danny Colquitt (half back), John Kneale (winger) and his brother Ernie (inside forward) - together they were a formidable squad and it was never an easy task to give Laxey a game at the Glen Road.

CHAPTER SEVEN

Dad's Passing

DAD'S business was doing well. He had established a good range of regular customers around the Laxey and Lonan area and his work had gained a lot of respect and admiration. A big step forward came when he won a contract to paint the first phase of the new estate being built for Douglas Corporation at Willaston. It was a major assignment and, for the first time, Dad had to have help in the form of two other painters whom he employed.

The houses were located in an area behind and close to the cemetery on Glencrutchery Road and it meant Dad had to get the bus to work each day instead of using his trusty bicycle around the village.

With Dad's success, the family prospered. Nick had started school at Laxey Primary and I had moved to Form 3A at St Ninian's High School which was the next level of education following Ballakermeen. I was still enjoying life as a scout.

Things were going well on the business front, but Dad's health had always been a concern and, during the summer of 1954, he became ill and had to be taken to Noble's Hospital for treatment. Worried about the Willaston contract, he suggested to his two col-

Dad loved motorcycling although he did not own a bike of his own. He marshalled at the TT at every opportunity.

leagues that, as he may be indisposed for some time, it would make sense for them to complete the work themselves. This was a big loss in income for Dad but, apparently, he felt it was the right thing to do.

The hospital treatment did not solve the problem and it was decided that the only way to a successful recovery for Dad was for him to undergo surgery.

The surgery was extensive and successful, but Dad's recovery seemed very slow and protracted. Suddenly there was a severe relapse and the doctors announced that Dad had contracted pneumonia. He never recovered.

Mum was distraught and at the age of thirteen, it was difficult for me to know what to say or what to do. The funeral was imminent and Mum decided that Nick and I should not attend as, in her opinion, we were too young to be subjected to the sombre event.

"It's much too serious for the two of you," she said, "I would much prefer you to go out on your bike, instead."

So I did. I was in Old Laxey near to the Post Office talking casually to a couple of friends of similar age when I was suddenly confronted by a couple of older guys, both of whom I knew, who demanded to know what I was doing.

"Just came out for a ride," I said.

"Disgusting." replied one of the guys, "You should be at your father's funeral!"

"But . . .," I started to explain, but just couldn't get the words out.

I was devastated to think that someone should be so mean as to say such a thing, but I was also greatly concerned that, in fact, they could be right. Did most people think the same?

I dashed home and waited for Mum and Auntie Ethel to come back from the funeral.

I related the conversation with the guy in Old Laxey.

"Take no notice," she said, "I preferred you not to go to the funeral and I believe I was right to do so."

Auntie Ethel and Nana seemed to agree and so the matter was dropped though I wondered for many years afterwards whether or not she was right . . .

As I got older, I wished that I had been more forceful with Mum and persuaded her allow me to attend - it would probably have been more fitting.

DAD'S passing was a life-changing moment for the Brown family.

Mum was left with no income to speak of and a thirteen-year-old and a six-year-old to raise. She decided there was no alternative - we had to move back to Nana's house at South Cape and she would have to find a job.

Moving back to "Briardale" was easy - well, relatively so, as Mum had

Nana and Auntie Ethel at "Briardale's" front gate. The house was an original Manx cottage which had been renovated around the turn of the century with a porch and a rear extension added. It still retained its outside "privy" however!

gathered together quite a few bits of furniture during our life on the Ramsey Road and, with the property being smaller and the family larger, a lot of re-arrangement was necessary at South Cape.

Finding work was rather different. Jobs were not easy to come by especially when there was a small family to take into account. We were fortunate that Nana and Auntie Ethel were there to assist and it enabled Mum to start work as a receptionist at Doctor Cunningham's surgery, just up the road from our home.

The working hours meant that she was able to be around for most of the time Nick and I were at home and, although the salary was not large, Mum gradually settled into a regular routine and began to enjoy life again.

For me, moving back to South Cape did not present a problem, but Peter Creer had left the Island to secure employment in England which meant that my "gang" was now more centred in the village.

The gang of rogues generally consisted of Geoff Rome, Tim Gilmore, Ken and Arthur Quine, my cousin Norman McKibbin, Allan Peake and a few others.

Most of our recreational time was spent on our bikes. We built a "dirt track" in the ruins of what was the old washing floors built originally for the Laxey Mine and which has now been converted into the Valley Gardens. We held races there regularly and in the summer months when Laxey was a popular tourist venue, tourists used to wait on the Main Road high above our dirt track for the bus back to Douglas.

The bus stop gave the tourists a grandstand view of our racing down below and we wised up to this quite swiftly. One of us would opt out of the cycling, walk up to the queue of people watching and pass round the hat for them to pay for the entertainment. It was magic! We were enjoying ourselves and getting paid for it! Most of us were able to keep our bikes in good repair as a result.

The cold winter evenings were often spent in the Laxey Workingmen's Institute which had a snooker table and an excellent dart board. Geoff Rome and I, together with some of the others, joined Laxey Rifle Club which had a range at the bottom of Baldhoon Hill. Prominent members at the time included Freddie Baxendale, then the company secretary at Laxey Glen Mills, Paul Dickenson, Harold Corlett, Johnny Rome - Geoff's Dad, John Scarffe and Eric Scarffe who was also heavily involved with the Workingmen's Institute.

SCHOOL had become a bit of a problem for me. As I was always the youngest, I found it increasingly difficult to keep up with the class in many subjects. Absence through illness also had an effect and when the results of the Third Form examinations were announced, I had performed badly.

I was devastated, but Mum was resolute. She decided that she would talk to the school about the situation and that meeting resulted in me staying in Form Three for an extra year and, instead of being the youngest in the class as previously experienced, I suddenly became the oldest. The move enabled me to catch up and I was very grateful to be given the second opportunity.

As a result, although I was never the brightest spark in the class, I did manage to perform regularly in the top half in most subjects with the exception of Latin which I especially loathed with a vengeance. I was in the last three for three separate Latin examinations - it's a good job I had no desire to be a doctor or a chemist!

I was of an age when a conversation often turned to my career. My Dad had always advised me to get qualified with a trade. "Anything but painting and decorating," he used to say.

My own desire for a number of years had been to follow my Grandad into the Royal Navy and when the recruiting office advertised for entrants, I sent for an application form.

However, it became obvious that any thoughts of leaving home for a life in the service would have to be discarded. Money was tight and Mum needed some additional family income.

She was shopping in Douglas one day and happened to bump into an old friend. The gossip must have turned to my future.

"Why don't you get him to apply to the newspaper for a job in printing - the timing may be opportune as they have just got a new owner . . .?"

CHAPTER EIGHT

Working for a Living

SO IN August 1956, I arrived at the back door of the *Isle of Man Times* building which, as the building extended from Athol Street through to Nelson Street, was located opposite Clague's Tripe Shop.

Harry Christian met me and introduced me to Ducket "Jackie" Lawson - my boss - and many of the staff who were to be my work colleagues for the next few years.

The composing room was a large area at the top of the newer part of the building built originally to house the new Cossar press installed in the basement in the late 1940s. Between the two areas was a floor which contained the bindery, the flatbed machine room and the boiler room. The three floors were accessed by way of a beautiful wrought iron circular staircase which, after a short while, could be traversed at great speed using the apprentices' "special technique" of sliding down the handrail!

The composing room contained eight Linotype machines - later increased to fourteen when the *Isle of Man Examiner* staff moved to the building - upon which operators converted into type the stories supplied by the journalists based in another part of the building. The type was a line of words - called a "slug" - which was formed by the operator tapping out sufficient words to form a line for the story and then "sending it away" to the casting section of the linotype where the "slug" was formed using molten metal. This section of the machine was automatically fed by a large ingot of type metal and the area was extremely hot - hot enough to keep your pies and pasties warm! A "splash" was often caused by a line not being fully wide enough, and could cause a severe burn to the operator. Thus, the machines were always treated with the greatest respect! The Linotype was a marvellous machine - yet another example of early German engineering. One of the machines that served in the *Times* office during my time there still remains in pristine condition on display in the foyer of Isle of Man Newspapers Limited in Peel Road.

My immediate "superior" was Ian "Flash" Wrigley who, with my arrival, was promoted to senior apprentice in the composing room. Flash took it upon himself to brief me on all the responsibilities of a junior apprentice: brushing the floor, running errands, proofing the typeset columns for reading, taking the completed formes to the Cossar press in the basement via the antiquated manual lift, amongst many others.

During the first year of my apprenticeship, I had to save hard in order to be part of a young "with-it" group who visited Liverpool to see one of the first showings of "South Pacific" in Panorama and travelled to Chester Zoo. Note the obligatory "fag"!

"You've also got to make the tea whilst I get the pies and pasties for the morning break," said Flash and I quickly became adept at making tea for around twenty in the large steel teapot which seemed to have been used for years.

After a few weeks, Flash was ill and didn't come in to work. Suddenly I was responsible not only for the tea but also running to Bateson's pie shop in Strand Street for morning sustenance for all the composing room staff.

Early on, Flash had given me the run-down on what was available from Bateson's and how much each item cost.

I sought an order from each member of staff:

"I'll have a pie, lad."

"Fine." I would say, "Do you want gravy?" Gravy was an additional one penny.

"Aye, please."

And off I went to Bateson's.

The order was placed - say, ten pasties, fifteen pies and gravy for nine.

"We haven't seen you here before - where's Flash?" said the very nice lady when I went for the first time.

"He's not well," I said.

"Mmmmm," was the knowing reply.

"Here you are, son. One pound four shillings and twopence, please," said the very nice lady.

I had done my own calculation based upon the prices Flash had given to me and I knew that she had undercharged me.

"I don't think you've charged for the gravy," I said.

"There isn't a charge for the gravy, son," she said.

I thought I had obviously got things wrong when I was instructed by Flash so, on the return to the *Times* Office, proceeded to pay back one penny to everyone who had ordered gravy.

"You did what?" said Flash when he returned to work a couple of days later. "That was my pay for doing the run each day."

Apparently the system was set up by one of his predecessors, Doug Baird, and had been in operation for a considerable time - Flash merely continued the arrangement, but it ceased from that day forward!

A week after my first day as an apprentice I was paid - in a small square envelope. I had previously said to Mum that I would bring my wages home to her and that she could take out her housekeeping needs from it and give me back the balance. When she opened the envelope the cash inside contained £1/19s. It didn't seem much at the time, but when you take into account the fact that a journeyman compositor who, it was generally considered, was well paid, earned around £12 a week, it was pretty good for the most junior of junior apprentices!

AT THE time, printing and publishing were two significant industries on the Isle of Man. The output ranged from the production of a few small business cards to the daily and weekly newspapers which were then published.

The Isle of Man Times Limited, a company originally founded in 1861 by James Brown who was jailed in 1864 for contempt of court, produced an edition of the *Isle of Man Daily Times* on Monday, Tuesday and Wednesday each week, and then the *Isle of Man Weekly Times* on Friday.

The *Isle of Man Examiner* founded in 1880 was published on Friday and its sports paper the *Green Final* was published on Saturday afternoon.

The *Isle of Man Courier*, a relatively young title first published in 1884, was published every Friday and the *Mona's Herald*, the oldest newspaper of them all dating back to the 1830s, came out on a Tuesday each week from its offices in Ridgeway Street, Douglas. The *Peel City Guardian* was rather erratic in its publication day but was a weekly issue - it was first published in 1884.

The printing firms comprised Bridson and Horrox, a family firm formed originally by Harry Horrox and his partner during the mid-1930s and based in elderly premises in Back Strand Street. They were a general printers but, as they had slightly larger equipment and a bigger staff, their production tended towards larger format work.

Norris Modern Press was originally formed by Samuel Norris, well-known in Manx political history, and was located in lower Victoria Street. It remained in the ownership of the Norris family.

Victoria Press was a small firm in third floor offices in upper Victoria Street. Nelson Press was also situated in Back Strand Street.

In Castletown, Les Edwards ran Castletown Press which he had formed during the 1930s, and "Paddy" Quine's, Quine & Cubbon, were in Port Erin. Fred Palmer ran Palmers in Peel where he published the *Peel City Guardian* and operated a small general printing office as well, and Maurice Strickett was in charge of the family firm of Stricketts in Parliament Street, Ramsey where he handled small print work and operated a stationers.

Some offices may have had just a couple of employees, whilst the main newspapers were staffed by over sixty trade union members and altogether some 300-350 Manx residents would have been employed in one way or another within the industry.

THE original *Times* Office composing room had quite a few characters. Linotype operator, Harry Christian was the elder statesman - he became a real father figure and a gentleman who was always ready to give good advice. Jackie Lawson, the foreman who, when he wanted the attention of the apprentices used to clap his hands and expect us to come running which, mostly, we did. Also on the Linotypes were Joe Cannell, recently returned from his National Service and an Isle of Man national football team winger, Brian Kneen and Des Hayward, who used to be a bus driver in the UK before moving to the Isle of Man. Allan MacLean was a compositor who, when he was not involved in the production of the newspaper, had a responsibility for the production of *Hansard*, the official record of the *Proceedings of Tynwald* which the *Times* Office were contracted to produce along with other general printing work.

Benny Howland was a linotype operator who joined the company from Victoria Press. Benny was a stickler for the rules and later when he was appointed Isle of Man Branch Secretary of the Typograhical Association - the union - he ran the branch with a rod of iron.

I recall one experience of Benny during the early part of my apprenticeship. On the Friday I was due to work on the *Green Final* in the afternoon of the following day and in company with one or two others, all journeymen, I was asked if I would go into work the following morning as well. Conscious of the overtime payment, I readily agreed.

When I arrived at the back door on Saturday morning I was met by Benny who asked me where I was going.

"To work, of course," I said, thinking he was joking.

"You're not!" says Benny. "Who told you to go to work on a Saturday morning?"

"Nobody told me, I was asked," and I suddenly realised he was serious. The other guys were pushing past to clock in and I was getting decidedly embarrassed.

"Did you mention it to the Father of the Chapel?" says Benny.

"No, I didn't realise I had to," rather lamely.

"Don't you realise that you will be doing the work a journeyman could be doing but at a much smaller cost to the company."

"I didn't think of it that way," I tried to explain as the thought of doing a journeyman out of work had suddenly made me not want to go in anyway. But that possibility was immediately dashed as well.

"Well, you'd better go in now that you are here," says Benny, "but make damn sure you don't get used like that again."

Apparently Benny lodged an official complaint with the management and a similar situation never arose again - it was quite a lesson to me and highlighted the power which the union held over the industry at that time.

JOHN Radcliffe was one of the older brigade. John had spent many years as a compositor until his eyes became bad. He was then moved to proof reading. How having bad eyes made this appropriate, I will never know?

The location of the proof readers' office was not one which would encorage good proof reading either. It was opposite the toilets which consisted of one urinal, two sit-down toilets and a wash basin. As smoking was not permitted in the composing room due to insurance restrictions relating to the wooden floor, the toilets were the only location for a quick fag - even though the floors were still wooden! As a result, at times as many as five or six could be squeezed into this area and the smoke was brutal.

John Radcliffe was a man of routine and he used to use the toilet for its main purpose at the same time every morning. He was also a man who obviously liked his food and its many variations and consequently the aroma during his visit was often very strong.

"Good God, John, what did you have for dinner last night?" was the normal response to him vacating the stall.

His answer was always the same, "Nothing special - anyway my **** don't stink - pure as the driven snow and sweet as a nut, it is!"

THE Cossar press in the basement, which fronted Nelson Street, was operated by Les Hewitt who was an excellent centre half on the books of St George's football club. Les had been responsible for the printing of the *Isle of Man Weekly Times* and the *Isle of Man Daily Times* for many years, but wasn't too happy about the impending move of *Isle of Man Examiner* into the Athol Street premises.

His concern was centred around the *Green Final* - the *Examiner's* sports paper which was published every Saturday afternoon and which, due to the lack of television coverage, many local folk depended upon to obtain the UK and local football results, so that they could properly check their football pools coupon. In those days, the newspapers were delivered by bus to out-of-town newsagents and I have seen many a queue forming outside a newsagent's on a Saturday afternoon waiting for the delivery from the passing bus of the shop's quota of *Green Finals*.

Les thought the move of the *Green Final* to his department may interfere with his Saturday game with St George's. As it happened, he was able to arrange things so that his own football was unaffected and he continued as boss of his Cossar domain.

I am indebted to Jill Quayle, who I knew in those days as Jill Evans and who worked in the bindery in the "Times" Office, for these two photographs. They are reproductions from a newspaper and so the quality is rather blurred.

(Top) Les Hewitt, right, operating the Cossar press assisted by Jill left and Ken Tomlinson.
(Below) Machine and bindery staff at the Miehle press - left to right, Arthur Quilliam, Eric Culpan, Heather Varley, Tommy Jennings, Jill, Ernie Corteen, Jim Moore, Stan Kewley and "Taffy" Williams.

CHAPTER NINE

Disaster

I GUESS there must be moments in everyone's life which remain, with startling clarity, in the mind for ever. 1958 threw up one for me. The apprenticeship was progressing very well - I was still the junior as there had been no additions to staff since I joined - but the work was enjoyable and I was gaining experience every day.

The *Times* Office, as well as being the production facility for the newspaper, also operated its own general printing department and, when I wasn't needed on the newspaper, I was able to learn about the composition of this work. Allan MacLean was always available for advice, as this area was basically in his charge, and because he too came from Laxey we struck up quite a good relationship.

In those days much of the general printing work was composed by hand, especially small jobs like business cards and letterheadings. The type was picked from a "case" which contained all the letters of the alphabet in varying sized boxes according to the usage of the alphabet character. Thus, an "e" was located in the largest box closest to the centre and characters like "q" and "z" were in the smallest boxes in the least accessible part of the case. There were hundreds of cases, stored in racks with a sloping top upon which the case could be rested, and each case contained a different type of typeface.

Allan managed to send some of the very basic work to me to tackle and so I learned how to make up a body of type in a "composing stick", how to "justify" it by hand - space out the lines so that each line in a column of type was the same width. I began to enjoy the work, especially when a little bit of design was required before the make-up of the job was undertaken.

The same principle of placing individual characters together to make words was used for the production of the "Daily Poster" which accompanied every parcel of newspapers delivered to the newsagents. They placed the poster in their display frame outside the shop and customers would then know the main story in that day's edition. A copy of the day's "poster" always appeared on either side of the *Times* building frontage in Athol Street.

This particular February day began as a perfectly normal day. The *Isle of Man Daily Times* was published on Mondays, Tuesdays and Wednesdays, and Friday was the publication day for the *Isle of Man Weekly Times*. It meant that Thursdays were invariably used to tidy things up after the three editions earlier in the week and to prepare for the weekly issue which was broadsheet, as opposed to the tabloid size of the "daily" editions and invariably contained a larger number of pages.

As the day progressed, it became increasingly obvious that something had happened. There were worried faces from the senior staff and especially from the reporters and editors. Bit by bit, news circulated of an aircraft crash in Lancashire. Apparently a visit had been arranged for motor dealers and associated suppliers to a UK battery company which would also involve a visit to a motor show.

An aircraft, a Bristol Wayfarer, part of the fleet belonging to Silver City Airways, had been used for the flight. It was originally a freight aircraft but it had been converted to accommodate passengers.

Without the present day instant news of television and, indeed a much less efficient radio service, details of the crash took a long time to reach the Island. Because of the journalists' connections with their UK counterparts, the *Times* Office seemed to be the only place where news was emerging.

A decision was made to publish an emergency edition of the paper and one, which contained esssentially as much information as had reached the office, was produced. It was rushed out and was gratefully received by a Manx public who were beginning to realise that the accident was in fact a disaster. It was obvious that follow-up editions would have to be produced and the end result was a total of four editions from late morning until early evening.

People began to gather in the newspaper's front office in Athol Street waiting for news as it came in. The reporters made regular trips from the editorial floor down to them to report on their findings. Part of my duties was to ensure that the two posters outside the front office were kept up to date with the contents of each issue and each time I had to change the posters I had to push through the crowd, many of whom by this time were very upset. It was an awful day! The ultimate toll resulted in twenty-three people directly connected with the Manx motor car industry losing their lives along with a further twelve whose connections with the industry were less involved. Seven survived the crash, including the Captain, First Officer and Stewardess.

The newspapers didn't have to seek out too much news for many weeks after the crash - the funerals, the follow-up stories and the questions as to how it had happened filled all the pages automatically and, of course, as they were the only real source of dependable news, all editions sold out.

CHAPTER TEN

Joining Forces

SOON afterwards, the move of the *Examiner* newspaper and its staff into the Athol Street premises took place and suddenly the composing room staff doubled in size. Two more apprentices joined the gang and I had two new mates - Michael Gilbertson and another chap called Colin.

Very quickly I found out that Colin's surname was Shaw. When I told my Mum about him she wondered if he lived in Hutchinson Square? When he confirmed the following day that he did, I announced, with a degree of pride, that he had been named after me and told him the story of our Mums being in the same ward at the "Jane".

What would be the odds on two people born within four days of each other, in the same place, with the same name, should both become apprentice compositors, work side-by-side and have a lifetime in the printing trade? I suggest they would be rather long!

Michael "Mitch" Gilbertson and Colin "Shortie" Shaw became life-long friends. The additional staff produced more characters: Dickie Clucas, foreman of the *Examiner* composing room - an imposing individual despite his small stature - could mix it with the best of them and we were to experience a few examples of Dickie taking on the Editor at press time. George Bradley was a lover of ballroom dancing. He and his wife were always in the thick of things when the ballroom dancing contests were held in Douglas. Victor Corlett was a compositor along with George. Dickie Craine, Bob McFee and Leslie Crellin - a very quiet, most introspective character - formed the nucleus of the newspaper typesetting team, along with Jim Pooley, Branch Secretary of the union, Eddie Skelly, Harold Cowin and Walter Cannell who later emigrated to New Zealand. Bert Reynolds and Laurence Kermode joined as comps, Eric Culpan moved into the machine room and on the Cossar Les Hewitt had been joined by John Shimmin and Jim Moore.

WHEN each completed newspaper page, now called a "forme", was ready for press, it was the apprentices' job to carry it to the lift and send it down two stories to the Cossar room so that the forme could be loaded onto the press.

At this point it's worth remembering that each forme consisted of eight newspaper columns, each around thirty inches long, made up with lines of type which had been produced on the Linotypes, loose type which was used for headings and lots of advertisements which consisted of type and illustrative blocks. Altogether, each forme prior to press represented an enormous amount of skilled work.

We used to take one forme between two of us as they were extremely heavy and the procedure was that, to ensure that the lift was not overloaded, no more than two formes were to be placed in it at any given time.

Things were running late one day, ominous noises were emanating from the Cossar Room as to whether or not the paper would be printed as no-one wanted to work overtime. The final four formes became ready at the same time. We carried three to the lift and decided to take a chance and put all four in at once.

"It'll be OK," said Flash. "I'll hold the rope and let it down slowly."

The load was far too heavy for him and, although we tried to grab the rope as well, the lift took off at an alarming pace and rocketed to the basement. Two of the formes were completely shattered and had to be re-assem-

Unfortunately, this photograph, taken at one of the staff annual dinners of the company, is damaged. However it is still possible to identify the following members of staff: Back Row - Brian Kneen (far left), Eric Gleave (next), Kevin Gleave (next), Donald Collings (next), Joe Cannell (next but one) and Ronnie Southall (next). Third Row from back left to right - Eddie Skelly (far left), Judy Corlett (next but one), May Callister (next, later my sister-in-law). Fourth Row from back left to right - Alan Bell (second left), Bill Dale (?), George Bradley. Front Row: Paul Kermode (centre).

bled. The paper was late and we got a severe bollocking - it never happened again!

THE journalists made regular appearances in the composing room. John Quirk, one of the senior staff who had his own feature column every Tuesday, had an air about him which scared the hell out of the apprentices. He was decidedly moody and could be very abrasive. Frank Roberts, was mostly seen at his desk in the reporters' room allegedly because he invariably was recovering from a previous evening's celebration. Tom Stafford, probably the least known to us, tended to spend most of his time in the reporters' room.

To the apprentices, Sean Kenny, a true Irishman if ever there was one, was always a target to whom proofs of typeset stories would be given for the purpose of checking them for literal errors and the like. Sean would give the proof the merest of glances and then sign his name to indicate that the article had been read. This, of course, was brilliant to save time when press time was approaching and so he was used extensively. Robert Kelly, later to become an excellent editor, was the junior reporter and the great Sydney Boulton joined the company in 1970 after a career in the *Ramsey Courier,* latterly as editor.

In addition to their normal reporting duties, all the reporters had to be part of the team which produced a verbatim report of Tynwald and the House of Keys business as the company had a contract with the Government to produce these reports called Hansard. The modern method is to use voice recognition and data transfer, but in those days the debates were recorded in shorthand and then typed out by the reporters, then typeset for a third time so that the reports could be printed and produced. As a result, invariably the reporters' shorthand capabilities were exemplary.

All of the reporters, and indeed the editors, enjoyed a trip downstairs to the composing room whenever possible. They were tightly controlled, however, by William "Billy" Bell - Alan's father - and Alice "Ally" Rylands - the joint editors. Willie was a very affable guy who had spent a lifetime in journalism, had reached the proverbial "top of the pole", and was quite happy to share stories with you if time permitted. Ally was a slightly different proposition - she was undoubtedly greatly experienced but was very severe in her attitude and certainly didn't suffer fools gladly. Both, unfortunately, retired not long after the takeover of the *Times.*

Eric Kinrade was the senior reporter in the *Examiner* team and the newspaper's editor was Curwen Clague. Curwen was a rather serious natured man but could also be particularly friendly, especially when a sports subject was being discussed. He was an excellent editor and was much admired by H L Dor, his new boss.

A few years later, when Curwen departed, Eric was appointed editor of the *Isle of Man Examiner* in his place. He proved to be an excellent choice and was strongly supported by a very good staff of journalists.

The machine room too had been boosted with new staff - Stan Kewley, a little man who was not afraid to punch well above his weight, was placed in charge of the general printing machine room. Arthur Quilliam, who had been part of the original *Times* set up as an apprentice, was joined by apprentice Tommy Jennings and journeyman Ernie Corteen. In the bindery, the elderly Ned Quiggin found himself with a new colleague in Heather Varley who was also often employed to hand feed the presses.

G. V. H. "Victor" Kneale, later to become a prominent member of Tynwald, used to make the plates which reproduced the photographs in the pages of the *Isle of Man Times*. Victor had been trained in the original style of platemaking which, in fairness, usually produced very good results for the time, but was a lot more time consuming for each plate made. At the time of the takeover, the *Examiner* had just installed a German machine to make plates at a faster rate. In essence, the Klischograph produced them within a matter of minutes whereas the original process would take hours. The end product was not as good and the eventual reproduction was not so clear, but time was of the essence. Unfortunately Victor had not been trained in the operation of a Klischograph and so his employment was terminated.

To his dying day, Victor never forgave H. L. Dor for making him unemployed. To many he had a very valid point and there was a lot of sympathy for him - he could have been retrained but Dor considered that two Klischograph operators would have been too many. Victor probably had the last laugh, however, when he went on to become a highly respected member of the Isle of Man Legislature instead!

BILLY Bell was a very approachable man, totally denying his most senior position on the newspaper. He was happy to talk to anyone and my interest in the local music scene, which was at that time just following the UK's explosion in that area, made me ask him if he would mind if I wrote a music column for the paper each week.

"Each week would be a bit much, lad," said Billy, "but I would consider a monthly feature. Why don't you write me a sample feature article and I'll make a decision based on that?"

I loved writing - always had no problems with English and essays in school - and so I jumped at the chance and "TeenBeat" was born and ran for three enjoyable years until I was near to the end of my apprenticeship. It also tied in very well with the regular visits I paid to the music club which had been assembled at the Anne Hathaway Cafe in Victoria Street. The club mostly concentrated on folk music but Tom Courtie and his band were regulars there along with John Harrison.

CHAPTER ELEVEN

Leisure and Learning

IN LAXEY, many of the "gang's" bicycles had been replaced by motorcycles and we were getting around the Island much more. I had managed to acquire a Matchless which had solid rear suspension, but had been converted for use as a trials bike. This meant that the front of the bike was particularly receptive to uneven terrain, but the rear was so solid that if you sat on the seat whilst negotiating a trials section you could end up with a black and blue 'bum'! Nevertheless, it made me mobile, didn't cost too much and therefore served an excellent purpose.

Living in a village at that time had its advantages. Television had not become the magnet it is to young people now and there were a number of clubs and associations to provide interest and challenges.

In addition to membership of the village football club Geoff Rome and I were also part of the Laxey Rifle Club and the Workingmen's Institute where there were very good snooker and billiards facilities. We joined the band of marshals which serviced the mountain section of the TT Course and mainly were stationed at what is now known as the Les Graham memorial but was, to us, the Stone Bridge.

Our membership of the Rifle Club invariably took us to "away" rifle matches once a fort-

We did our share of marshalling for the TT and the MGP. Allan Peake and Geoff Rome, suitably garlanded, at the Graham Memorial.

night during the winter. The matches were, in the main, a social event for most of the team and a lot of time was always spent in the adjacent pub. The singing in the coach on the way home was always a joy and there were some very good voices scattered around, in particular John Scarffe whose rendition of *Jerusalem* was always well received.

We had progressed in the football club as well. Geoff and I were now regulars for the Combination League team - the reserves - and we usually turned out each Saturday. Geoff had secured work in a radio and TV shop in Ramsey and Tim Gilmore joined the staff of the Flour Mill at Laxey. Norman McKibbin, my cousin, had begun work at Manx Engineers

We had all reached an age where members of the opposite sex became more than a bearable nuisance. There were a number of very attractive Laxey girls and they suddenly became part of our coterie. It became noticeable that part of the gang would disappear for a few hours, and "not be able to make it tomorrow - got a date!"

We were not too happy with the regular invasion of Douglas lads who, it appeared, viewed the girls of Laxey as a very nice alternative to those available in their own vicinity. However, it wasn't all one way traffic. Flash and I had become friends with a mixed group in Douglas and often enjoyed get togethers and visits to the cinema. I particularly recall a day trip to Liverpool to to see the film "South Pacific" which was shown in the new sensational format of "Panorama"!

Flash never ceased to amaze me - when we all became interested in motor-cycles we met at regular intervals, often at the coffee bar on Onchan Head where the juke box, with all the tunes of the day, was available.

One such day, out of the blue, whilst we were all lounging around at the bar, Flash arrives - not on any old "bike" but on a brand new Ariel Leader which, in its day, was revolutionary as it was the first every-day motor-cycle to have a fully enclosed engine and a streamlined fairing. Of course it meant that Flash had the girls begging for him to give them a pillion ride on this great bit of kit. How he did it, I will never know, but he did.

Life with Flash was hectic. We tried hard not to do overtime on Saturday mornings in the summer because that was when Ivy Benson's Band used to hold jive sessions in the Villa Marina. It was also the time for changeovers in the boarding houses with new tourists arriving - and girls setting foot on the Island and looking for entertainment!! It was great and we had the time of our lives. We enjoyed visits to the Majestic Hotel where each table in the bar was equipped with a telephone - great for asking a girl to dance - or not, as the case may be! We frequented Pennington Hall in Onchan where the weekly jive sessions offered a wonderful display of ladies legs! Dancing was available everywhere - Palace Ballroom, Villa, Palais de Danse and regular organised events at all the local hotels.

Liverpool Branch of the TA hosted a contingent of members of the Isle of Man Branch of the Guild of Young Printers seen here leaving Ronaldsway. Left to right: Paul Kermode, Henry Moorhouse, Ffinlo Crellin, Colin Shaw, Roger Oram, Michael Gilbertson, myself, Tommy Jennings and Arthur Quilliam.

Guild
of
Young
Printers
Visit to
Liverpool

Posing elegantly whilst enjoying some type of beverage!! Colin Shaw, Roger Oram, Arthur Quilliam, myself and Tommy Jennings, both with headwear!

The visit included a excellent dinner which was organised and attended by the Liverpool Branch Secretary, Fred Wharton.

LIFE was, indeed, enjoyable but I was a bit concerned about my apprenticeship. We were all part of the Guild of Young Printers - a junior branch of the Typographical Association - and were affiliated to the Liverpool Branch.

With fares underwritten by the Isle of Man Branch of the union, a number of the Isle of Man Guild paid a visit to Liverpool where we were hosted by the Liverpool Branch and the Liverpool Branch Secretary of the Typographical Society, Fred Wharton. Quite an enjoyable trip it was, too.

The association with Liverpool meant that we were kept informed of most of the Guild's activities in the area as well as all the apprenticeship qualification requirements. It became apparent that in that area all apprentices went to the city's College of Art for one day each week under the day-release scheme negotiated between the employers there and the union. This enabled them to sit an examination for the Certificate of the City and Guilds of London Institute - a highly recognised body of training standards.

Whilst I was gaining knowledge every day from my older work colleagues, I knew that a proper apprenticeship should include the City and Guilds Certificate at the end and so I began to make enquiries as to how I could achieve it.

The local College of Art, in Kensington Road, was offering classes for "printed art". They were run by Norman Sayle and Eric Houlgrave, both highly respected in the field of art within the Island. The classes ran on one night each week and on a Saturday morning and I decided to sign on, along with a few of the other lads in the office, and there were one or two apprentices from other print offices as well.

It wasn't easy for Norman Sayle and Eric Houlgrave. Whilst they had no problem covering the elements of graphic design, they were also trying to teach the basics of an industry of which they themselves had only a very elementary knowledge and on many occasions their lack of experience in the trade let them down. This meant that some of the guys lost interest and just didn't bother to turn up.

I bought some books on printing and one, in particular, was promoted by the Typographical Association in order to encourage people to join the industry. I quite enjoyed the classes at the college and gained quite a bit of knowledge from my newly-acquired books on the trade.

At the end of the college year, those of us who had stuck it out sat our City and Guilds First Year examination. There was no practical work involved - it was a purely written examination - but I was very pleased to receive notification that I had passed.

Attendance at night school meant that some of the leisure activities had to be curtailed, however, football and rifle shooting were still a big part of my life.

CHAPTER TWELVE

Expansion

THE MOVE of the *Examiner* into the offices of the *Times* at Athol Street went further than merely increasing the printing staff. The new owner - Henrie Leopold Dor, a rather mysterious person to us juniors - was reputed to be part of a very wealthy family based in the South of France.

We were told they owned large areas of vineyards and were highly respected in the region. This particular aspect of his life was supported later on when his family decided to sell their interests in the France. Much of the estate and its contents were put up for auction and the catalogue for the auction was enormously thick and presented in full colour - rather abnormal for the time.

His business history was similarly somewhat mysterious. It was thought that he had connections in the Mediterranean area, mainly Malta, but despite investigation nothing could be uncovered.

Dor was married but we never laid eyes on his wife - she apparently did not care for the Isle of Man and preferred to live in their apartment at Hyde Park Gate in London. He was an active member of the Atheneum - a highly respected private members' club in Mayfair.

"HL", as he became known, seemed to have some strange aspects to his life. He raved about the artwork of Matisse, for example - in my elementary way, I thought his stuff was dreadful - and he appeared fascinated with astrology and all things concerned with foretelling the future. Typically, he introduced a column as part of the newspaper which purported to have been written by his pet sheepdog "Strog". The column became a source of ridicule, to those involved in the newspaper, especially the reporters.

HL's right-hand man was Herbert Quayle. Herbert was a likeable manwho had worked for the Radcliffe family, the previous owners of the *Examiner*, prior to enlisting in the Manx Regiment and serving throughout the second world war, mainly in Ethiopia and Eritrea.

When peace returned, Herbert returned to the Island and was made

Manager of the *Examiner* by the Radcliffes. Thus he was in position when HL became interested in the acquisition and it was said at the time that the preservation of Herbert's position in the company was part of the deal Dor made with the Radcliffes.

Anyway, Herbert became the Manager of the new, combined operation which followed the move to Athol Street and, apparently as part of the brief given to him by HL, he set about expanding the printing division of the company as well as developing the newspapers.

I still had a couple of years left of my apprenticeship, but when the management introduced a regular magazine to the production schedule, I was asked to take on the page make-up. Obviously, I wasn't going to miss such an opportunity, it was a big step up, and I grabbed it with both hands. It turned out that the magazine was called *Fate* and had been secured for the company by HL. It was a small format publication which, to me, contained utter nonsense, but it is still in circulation today!

Herbert Quayle had quite a few good connections in the publishing world in London and he set about bringing some of their publications to the company for production. Quite soon we had a few monthly titles to turn out not the least of which was the very risqué *Health and Efficiency*. It was not quite as explicit as most mens' magazines are these days as all of the areas around the models delicate parts had to be airbrushed, but the fact that it was being printed in the Isle of Man certainly raised a few eyebrows.

New equipment had been purchased for the machine room which enabled the printing of eight "quarto" magazine pages at a time and folders were bought to support the new gear. This upgraded the facilities substantially and probably contributed to one of the management's biggest boobs.

WITH news of the expansion and the upgrading of equipment leaking out, the company persuaded the Isle of Man Tourist Board that we could "easily" produce the *Isle of Man Tourist Guide*. At the time the print run was in the region of 400,000 copies per year, contained some 140 pages and was produced by Jarrold's of Norwich - one of the UK's largest printers using rotary presses which could print sixteen colour pages at 20,000 copies per hour.

The whole exercise was destined for failure from the start. There was no proper timetable for the supply of copy for advertisements and for editorial, consequently pages were continually altered and the whole of the pre-press work was a mess.

When the completed formes eventually reached the pressroom for printing, the enormity of the task finally struck home! The new equipment, though quality for its time, could only run at about 5,000 sheets per hour for each eight pages to be printed. After that the printed sections had to be folded and the folders ran at about 3,000 per hour.

There were probably more arguments over working overtime on the *Guide* than any other job produced in the company whilst I was there. Eventually, after all sorts of new shift patterns and regular overtime, the job was completed and delivered but massively, massively late and Len Bond, who was the Director of Tourism, at the time was far from happy!!

The production of the *Guide* was never considered a target for a long while after that.

THE relatively famous *Farmers Weekly* was a newspaper-format publication which kept the agricultural trade informed in detail about the prices which they obtain for their crops and livestock.

As the title suggests, the publication was weekly and had been produced in London for many years. The pages which covered the crop and livestock prices were fundamental to the whole publication and made up most of the content. They were very detailed, much like the stock market prices in the *Financial Times*, and they certainly could not be produced using the Linotype system in the *Times* office.

Herbert Quayle's London contacts, however, offered the work to him and he set about exploring how it could be taken on. He was advised that the only way to produce the "prices" pages was to install a Monotype system. This was a system of typesetting which, instead of producing lines, or "slugs" of type as for the newspaper, produced individual characters of type but in line formats. This made the weekly amendment of the prices relatively easy to accomplish.

The problem was that nobody on the printing staff of the company knew the first thing about Monotype. It was obvious, therefore, that skilled staff would have to be employed to handle the work.

Neil Clarke arrived and supervised the installation of two Monotype machines. Neil was from the south of England and was keen to advance his career. He saw the opportunity in the Isle of Man as a step up - he would, virtually, be his own boss, and he would be in the fortunate position of being the only employee in the company who could handle the work.

Whilst Neil looked after the monotype production, there was still a requirement for a compositor to handle its output and to supervise the pagination of the production. Allan MacLean was identified as the ideal candidate, mainly due to his excellent and detailed work on the Hansard reports, and with a degree of trepidation he took on the responsibility.

It is doubtful that Neil Clarke ever realised the work which was to be involved in the production of *Farmers Weekly*. Whilst Monotype was the perfect medium from which to produce the prices pages, the actual work involved in changing the prices, the time restraints within which he had to work, the continual need for accuracy and the more careful handling which

Monotype demanded, all made the whole exercise very difficult both for him and for Allan.

Still, they persevered and the publication continued to be published in the office for a number of years until it changed hands and the contract was eventually terminated.

AT home, Mum announced that she was to get married again.

She had been seeing John Duggan for quite some time and so the news was not a great surprise to me. What was important was her happiness and John appeared to go a long way towards filling the gap left in her life when Dad died. I was very happy about it.

John lived with his family in a large family home on the long straight between the top of the Whitebridge Hill and the Liverpool Arms. He was employed by the Highway Board as a ganger on the

Mum and John on their wedding day.

road, but he was waiting for an opportunity to follow his father who had served on the Manx Electric Railway for a very long time.

They eventually got married on Christmas Eve 1959 and I was delighted to be asked to give my Mum in marriage. John joined the M.E.R shortly afterwards and stayed with them until his retirement.

CHAPTER THIRTEEN

It's amazing who you meet on a bus!

THE ONLY painful parts of the working day were the journeys to and from Laxey on the bus. I had to revert to using the buses as I had managed to write off my motor-cycle in an accident one morning at Rosemount crossroads in Douglas.

I had just picked up Ernie Corteen as a pillion passenger at York Road and we were just half a mile or so from the office. The morning was wet, though it wasn't raining hard but the roads were greasy.

Approaching Rosemount, I suddenly saw a van emerging from Windsor Road - there was no way I could get round him and I just put the bike down. Unfortunately, Ernie went flying over my head, I went to the left and the bike went to the right ending up under a Corporation double decker which was parked outside Rosemount Church.

Ernie and I were both unhurt - I had a scratch on my cheek where, presumably, I had hit the road, but we were both very fortunate. The same couldn't be said for the bike. The whole right side of the machine had been damaged and the bus had done a bit more to it, just to make sure.

Eventually, I was able to take what was left of the bike to the motor-cycle garage, then in Fort Street. They took one look at it, shrugged their shoulders and said "Don't expect too much". They did agree that they would get it surveyed by the insurance, however. The end result was that I was offered £40 for the bike for scrap! The damn thing was insured for more than that but that was all I got.

I never did understand how the van driver actually got away with it. I recognised the van and reported how everything had happened to the police when they arrived on the scene. The van driver had driven on, presumably unaware that he had been the cause of an accident. I didn't hear again from the police and no charges were made.

My new step-father was the proud possessor of an ancient flat tank bike which had a manual gear change on the tank. Nowadays, it would have been worth a small fortune as a relic. John thought the world of the thing - I thought it was bit of rubbish, however, it was a method of getting around and I had my eye on it.

I eventually persuaded John to let me take the thing for a spin. He agreed providing he could be a pillion passenger.

We set off on the Douglas road and were doing quite well as we approached Ballacannell Manx Electric Railway crossing.

I just did not see the tram crossing the road, and if it hadn't been for the agonised yell to stop from John, we would both have ended up underneath it.

That was enough for John - I didn't get to ride the thing again. Maybe I was just fated not to be a motor-cycle rider, or at least not a successful one.

SO I went back to the buses. The morning bus left Laxey at 7.15am and arrived in Douglas at 7.50 - just in time for me to get up to Nelson Street to clock in at 8am. If it was late which, in fairness, was very seldom, I had to have some reason for a late clock time but there were ten minutes of leeway before you risked having your wage docked.

The evening service left the Douglas bus station at 5.20pm. Both buses were invariably full but the evening one was by far the worst as it had to cope with shop workers as well as office workers who all finished work at around the same time, and on occasions, they put on an extra bus to cope with the traffic.

I finished at 5pm which gave me time to walk down to the station and get in the queue early. After a while, I became aware of a very attractive young lady travelling home every evening and also alighting at South Cape.

Investigations revealed that her name was Gwynneth Cregeen. She worked in the Education Authority main

Gwynneth - 1958.

Shortly after I met her, Gwynneth became 'Queen of Sport' in a contest at the Villa Marina.

offices in Strand Street - on the first floor of what is now the Regent Street Branch of Isle of Man Bank - and she had recently been in the "Miss Isle of Man" contest at the Villa Marina and got into the final six. Previous to that, I was told, she had been crowned "Castletown Festival Queen". I thought she was lovely but was very nervous about chatting her up.

Glory be! A marvellous opportunity presented itself when she had to sit alongside me one night. We chatted amiably enough but I still couldn't get it out of my head that here was a beauty queen and it was made even worse when she mentioned that she had been nominated for the "Queen of Sport" title which was imminent.

We got off the bus and our conversation continued for a short while - until I suddenly asked if she would like to go out one night. To my surprise she agreed - and that was another life changing moment!

CHAPTER FOURTEEN

A close shave

W E "went steady" for some two years before the wedding but I had known straight away that she was the one for me and I had asked her to marry me after six weeks! Gwynneth's Dad had spent his life with a strong connection to the sea. He was employed for many years by the Isle of Man Steam Packet Company and, when he felt he needed to spend more time at home with his family, he became a Harbourmaster.

He had been stationed at Castletown for a few years and was now Harbourmaster at Laxey which was still a working harbour for the coasters of Ramsey Steamship Company delivering bulk flour for Laxey Glen Mills and coal for a merchant in Glen Road. Edwin's role also included him deputising for other harbourmasters around the Island when they had their day off.

Edwin Cregeen could be very gruff at times, but underneath was kind and generous to his family. He and Annie had married late in life and Annie was in her 'forties' when Gwynneth was born. Edwin originated from the south of the Island and Annie was a Laxey/Lonan girl, although it became apparent to me that Annie, in particular, had relatives all over the Island.

I became a regular at Harbour House - especially for Sunday lunch - and there was an incident quite early on in our courtship which made me question whether I was doing the right thing.

Edwin was a swarthy character - Gwynneth has always claimed he has Spanish ancestry - but his appearance was one which would seem natural

Annie and Edwin Cregeen - whilst it was impossible not to fall in love with Annie, Edwin had me worried for quite a while, but we eventually became the best of friends.

One of our first dates - in Ramsey.

for a guy who had spent the major part of his life at sea. He sported a grand head of black "thatch" which, even in later life, never seemed to include a grey hair. This Sunday, he was standing in front of the mirror in the living room using the electric shaver so that he was presentable for lunch.

"It's a bloody nuisance this shaving," he announced to me, "twice a day, every day."

He looked at me.

"I bet you don't have to do it as often as that," he suggested. "How many times do you shave?"

This was exactly where I was hoping the conversation would not go.

"Well, actually, I don't really shave yet - I only have to do it a few times a month."

Edwin's mouth fell open.

"What?" he shouted. "Gwynneth!"

Gwynneth was in the kitchen helping her Mum with the lunch but dashed into the living room to see what her Dad was on about.

"What kind of a fella are you marrying here, Gwynneth?" he asked with a very straight face. "He doesn't even shave yet!"

I think he was joking - anyway the incident was completely ignored by Gwynneth and her Mum but I was none too happy and it made me very wary of Edwin for some time.

GEOFF Rome and I were playing for Laxey in 1960 when the club celebrat-

Proud winners of the 1961 Junior Cup - Laxey AFC Combination: Left to right, back row - Jimmy Gordon, Allan Cannell, Michael Scarffe, Johnny Gilmore, John Cowin, Roddy Jones. Front row - Geoff Rome, Peter Kinnish, myself, Michael Gilmore and Ernie Cleator.

ed its Jubilee with a dance and whist drive in the Glen Gardens where a certain "Queen of Sport" presented prizes during the evening..

During the following season, we were mostly given runs out in the Combination side and were doing quite well in the Combination League - we

A celebration for the Junior Cup winning Laxey AFC with many of the cup-winning team in attendance including myself, sitting left front next to my Auntie Myra and opposite Johnny Gilmore, Ronnie Smith, Geoff Rome and Jimmy Gordon. Behind them Peter Kinnish and Michael Gilmore and, at the back Michael Scarffe, Ernie Cleator, Rod Jones and John Cowin.

were challenging for the title and were still in the Junior Cup - a trophy then set aside for the reserve teams. In their wisdom the club had made me captain of the Combination side. I think the real reason was that they were of the view that my couple of runs out in the first team was about all I could ever expect and therefore it made sense to appoint a regular member of the "Combi"!

We missed out on the title by one point, but we did get to the Junior Cup Final which was played at the relatively new Bowl - and won! We beat Peel 1-0 and it was quite an achievement as the Peel team were heavily fancied to win. It was the one and only time I was presented with anything on behalf of any team and I was as proud as punch! A riotous night was had by all!!

Many of the Junior Cup-winning team played in the Cowell Cup final the same year and won that as well when they beat Peel again - 3-2.

Most of my friends were now in the Douglas area and the following season I joined Douglas High School Old Boys. Michael Gilbertson, his twin brother, Peter and Colin Shaw all played for them and all were selected a number of times for the Island squad. Peter Clague, my school chum of years ago was also part of DHSOB and he too represented the Island.

As well as these guys, club captain Geoff Clague, goalie Mike Corris and Kenny Gilbertson who was Michael and Peter's elder brother, were all Island "internationals", and so the club could boast some class!

I had a few outings with the Combination side and then injuries to regular players brought about my selection for the first team in the semi-final of the Railway Cup against Castletown at their stadium. Castletown was an in-form team and their supporters were very vocal and very loyal.

I was nervous - I was playing out of position at right back and the Castletown winger I had to mark was fast, very fast. At half-time we had held them despite a couple of scares, and Geoff Clague went to each player to offer support.

"You are doing well. I know he's fast," he said to me, "but don't forget, he falls the same as everyone else!"

I took this to mean I needed to tackle stronger and so in the first ten minutes of the second half I downed the guy way out on their left flank. The referee called a foul, which I thought was wrong, but still the kick could be dangerous and it was with some relief to me when we managed to clear our lines.

Strangely, Geoff's comment was right on the button - the fast winger didn't provide much trouble after that. Within the last ten minutes we scored and then held out for the win - the crowd were not happy!

It was nice to hear the Captain remarking how pleased he was with the performance of the replacement right back. It didn't do me much good, though, I didn't make the team for the Final.

CHAPTER FIFTEEN

An Offer worthy of Acceptance

THE fact that we were now a couple meant that my whole lifestyle changed - instead of having single guys and girls as friends, their place was taken by married and engaged couples. Michael Gilbertson had met Irene Chatel and they were a pair, Colin Shaw had met Margaret Haggerty and they were going steady. We often met up with Joe Cannell and his wife Jean, and Les and Kay Hewitt and so the circle of friends grew.

Unfortunately, it meant that the close association I had enjoyed with many of the gang in Laxey loosened quite a bit and most of the guys went their own way. My long-time mate Geoff Rome had met Thelma Surridge from Ramsey and they appeared destined for a life together.

I was due to finish my apprenticeship shortly after my twenty-first birthday and we arranged that our wedding would take place the year after so that I could at least be a journeyman when we set up home together.

In addition, I was still studying for City and Guilds in printing but any qualifications could only apply to oral work - there simply were no facilities available on the Island to enable anyone to reach the full standard.

Herbert Quayle must have heard about the complaints I was making to the rest of the staff about this and, out of the blue, he approached me to enquire how things were going at night school.

"Well, as good as they are able, Mr Quayle," I replied.

"But you do have a problem?" he asked.

So I told him all about it.

He asked a lot of questions and seemed genuinely interested.

"Leave it with me . . ," he said, mysteriously.

"Leave it with me" was a common saying that had become synonymous with the management not agreeing with a request made to them and employing a delaying tactic.

I thought . . . yeah, right, that's the last I'll hear of that!

A week later I was called into Herbert Quayle's office and told that it had been arranged for me to spend the final six months of my studies work-

In 1961 we were Chief Bridesmaid and Best Man for our friends, Michael Gilbertson and Irene Chatel seen here with me at Tynwald Hill on a weekend outing.

ing full-time with the instructors at the Printing Department of the College of Art in Hope Street, Liverpool. This would enable me to get sufficient study time to sit all of the Final examinations of the City and Guilds certificates in all of the printing and associated trade studies.

And the company would continue to pay my wages in full whilst I was in Liverpool!

Absolutely tremendous news! I was very grateful and determined at that moment that I would succeed in my attempts to get the best possible qualifications.

It meant that I had to find accommodation for six months but that problem was swiftly solved when a brother of my step-father offered me a room in their home at Speke.

I SPENT the first six months of 1962 in Liverpool. It materialised that Herbert Quayle had organised the whole thing with the College Principal and the arrangement was the first of its kind for the College.

It was good to be able to properly study, to gain practical experience of the various aspects of printing, to share the experience with other lads of the same age and with experienced professionals who were skilled in passing on their knowledge to others. The equipment at the College was wide ranging and my instructors made sure that all aspects of the course were covered including graphic design and basic print management. At times, I was alone in the class and able to have a one-to-one with the instructor. There were visits to a paper making plant and another to a manufacturer of printing inks.

The leisure time was excellent, too! The college was in Hope Street just a few paces from the Philharmonic Hall and, more importantly, the Philharmonic pub. We spent many lunch hours in the pub listening mainly to folk music from a number of artists who became well-known in later life. So much so that a few times we fell foul of the College's instructors when we returned late for the afternoon session.

John Lennon had been a student at the Liverpool College of Art a couple of years before me and he, along with another student Stuart Sutcliffe, had formed a group which performed regularly around the Liverpool area. They had just decided to call themselves "The Beatles" and became a regular turn at the Cavern Club in the city centre - the evenings were especially good there. The Cavern was a great place - once you had pushed your way past the rubbish bins located in the alleyway of an entrance - and it was invariably packed. We also went to see Gerry and the Pacemakers and a number of other local groups who were starting out in the growing music scene in Liverpool.

In May, we all sat our City and Guilds examinations. The number varied according to which aspect of the industry you were studying. I sat five - General Printing Theory, General Printing Practice, Compositor's Work, Graphic Design, and Printing Management.

In return for Herbert Quayle's efforts, I really wanted to do well and returned to the *Times* Office with a certain amount of trepidation and a large amount of hope.

There were other matters to hand, however, as planning for our nuptials had already begun some months previously . . .

GWYNNETH had set about organising things and planning the "do". It was decided very quickly that we would get married in Christ Church which is situated in the Laxey Manx Electric Railway station. The setting is quaint - and still is, in fact - we both liked the church and, in my younger days, I had been an irregular attendee of their Sunday School for many years.

My Mum had been doing some part-time work at the Glen Hotel in Laxey and they offered to put on a ham salad tea reception for us - the charge was to be twelve shillings per head.

There were quite a few marriages at the time. Gwynneth and I had acted as chief bridesmaid and best man at the wedding of Michael and Irene Gilbertson in 1961 and we were still many months from the big day when we both attended the marriage of a close friend who had a reception at the Derbyhaven Hotel, at that time run by Mr Peter Pahn.

The reception was impressive - a full dinner, the whole of the hotel at their disposal, dancing and a lovely garden next door for photographs. We became rather interested and made enquiries as to cost. Mr Pahn said he would do exactly the same for us on 8 September for seven shillings and sixpence.

Prior to working in the newspaper, I had been doing some part-time work for A & R Caine's Garage in Laxey - mainly just running messages and filling cars with petrol. It was actually just to earn a bit of pocket money. A chance conversation with them over the possibility of hiring one of their coaches to take guests to Derbyhaven resulted in them offering to do it for nothing for us!

That clinched it! All change - Glen Hotel out - Derbyhaven in. The Glen Hotel were not pleased but we felt that we were perfectly justified in switching as we got better value and saved a lot of money for Gwynneth's family at the same time.

At the time, it was normal procedure for couples to have a chat with the vicar prior to the wedding. Some six weeks beforehand, we arranged to see him at the Vicarage and duly turned up for our interview. We were met by the vicar's wife and ushered into the front room - we sat there for quite a while.

The vicar eventually came in, shook hands and sat opposite.

"Now you are about to set out on a journey together and there are a few points we need to clarify," he said.

"Firstly, I am marrying two people, aren't I," he enquired, "not three?"

The implication went over my head but Gwynneth was ready for it.

"Yes, you are marrying two people, " she said quite tartly. "I'm not pregnant."

I couldn't believe what he had said . . . but it got worse . . .

"Now you must understand," he said, "that once you are married, you are free to have sex whenever you wish and wherever you are. My wife and I, for example, often decide that we will have sex in the middle of the afternoon."

It was difficult to keep a straight face and we couldn't get away quickly enough from the remainder of the so-called pre-wedding interview. We laughed as we walked all the way back to Gwynneth's home next to the harbour at Laxey but our hilarity soon evaporated when we related the events to her Mum and Dad.

"Well, you needn't think I'm going to his church," said Edwin with a vengeance. "It's disgusting - talking to people like that. Who does he think he is? I'll go and sort him out!"

We managed to calm him down, but he was adamant that he would not be attending any marriage at which "that fella" was officiating. The success of our forthcoming marriage was in jeopardy.

In later years we had a wry smile when we saw that this vicar had been appointed to Relate - the organisation which helped couples having difficulties with their marriage . . . we often thought it would be intriguing to know what his contribution would be when couples were interviewed!!

CHAPTER SIXTEEN

Marriage Message

IT WAS part of Edwin Cregeen's make-up that he tended to fly off the handle at the drop of a hat, then after a relatively short while become conciliatory.

His job as Harbourmaster meant that he controlled the mooring of all small boats in what was, in effect, a working harbour.

Garwick Sailing Club had just been formed. Their headquarters were in Laxey and the main base for their yachts was Laxey Harbour.

Edwin did not like yachts or yachtsmen.

His Merchant Navy background and this dislike, coupled with the need to keep the harbour free for the "Ben" boats, meant that he was often at odds with the yachtsmen who, in Edwin's view, took a great delight in purposefully mooring their vessels in those specific parts of the harbour needed for the merchant vessels.

His temper was strained on many occasions when, in his view, "those bloody yachtsmen" had to be sorted out.

However, his return to an even temper was normally quite swift and Gwynneth and I experienced this over the wedding and his annoyance with the vicar.

And so we proceeded towards our September date with a lot less worry.

In August, the results of the City and Guilds examinations were announced. Fortunately I had done

I had managed to do quite well in my City & Guilds examinations - the local union branch decided it was noteworthy and I was presneted with a gift by the President, Eric Culpan.

quite well with passes in all subjects and distinctions in three of them. I was happy to pass on the information to Herbert Quayle and I believe I saw a slight smile of satisfaction.

A STAG night in those days traditionally was arranged for the night before a guy's wedding. The main aim appeared to be to get the prospective bridegroom so drunk that he would have difficulty performing without causing laughter next day at the ceremony.

We had developed quite a good relationship with the Derby Castle Hotel. The licensee was the mother of a former classmate of mine at the

Two upright young men - Michael and I arrive early.

The wedding party, left to right: Colin Shaw (groomsman), Eric Scarffe, Ann Cregeen (bridesmaid), Edwin Cregeen, Annie Cregeen, Groom, Bride, Mum, John Duggan, Nick, Irene Gilbertson (maid of honour) and Michael Gilbertson (best man). In front: Sarah, Anne and Bridget Cousins (bridesmaids).

High School, Bernie May, and a number of us used the pub regularly.

Mrs May, when she heard of my impending marriage, would hear of nothing other than us having my stag night at her pub. I must admit that I believe it was a good night and that she provided a really good buffet for us. I have no idea if that was, in fact, the case as I remember nothing after around 9pm.

Our car was halted by a rope across the road. It was a tradition in those days for newly-married couples to "pay" the children to get past.

I am told that I was brought home to Laxey and poured into the house by my "mates". Mum told me that I went straight to bed and that she was concerned about how I would be the following day.

As it happens, although at times I felt a bit "fuzzy", I was well up for the wedding and everything was OK.

The event went off without a hitch. The vicar behaved admirably and Gwynneth's Dad turned up!

The church was full and there was quite a crowd outside to see us emerge as man and wife. We had to experience the Manx tradition of giving pennies to the kids when a rope was stretched across the road in front of the wedding car, and we then had a lovely drive to Derbyhaven, stopping at my home at South Cape so that my bedridden Nana could see Gwynneth in her wedding finery.

After the celebrations at Derbyhaven, we headed for the airport to fly out that evening to Dublin. The guests decided they were going to see us off on our honeymoon - as a result the airport was very lively. We disappeared rather quickly through "Departures" - the guests, however, were determined that the party would go on and decided that they would continue to celebrate with the coach stopping at the Lancashire Hotel until closing time!

The following morning in Dublin, we were just finishing breakfast in the Four Courts Hotel when over the intercom there was a request for me to attend the front desk for a message. Thinking it would be the car hire firm delivering the vehicle, I dashed out smartly.

In those days a telegram was delivered by a telegraph boy who normally waited until the message was read in case a reply was needed and he had to deal with it.

A telegraph boy stood by the reception desk which was manned by three of Dublin's finest young ladies.

"Mr Brown?" he enquired. I nodded.

"A message for you, sir," he said. And he waited.

I opened the message with the full knowledge that all three girls were watching carefully. I had a feeling that they had experienced a situation like this on more than one occasion in the past.

The message was from all of those "mates" of mine from the *Times* Office who attended the wedding. It could not possibly have been any more explicit or suggestive and, despite my attempts to infer that the message had great business significance, I couldn't help a small smile.

"Will there be any reply, sir," I had forgotten that the telegraph boy was there.

"No, no, I don't think it requires a reply," I said offering a coin at the same time.

I swear I heard the reception girls' giggles!

The hire car arrived and we set off for County Sligo, my Nana's birthplace, as the first port of call on the drive around Ireland which we had been planning for months.

We arrived at the only hotel I had previously selected for the trip. My intention was to seek out the others as we drove around. The Yeats Country Club was just outside Tubbercurry, my Nana's home village.

I presented myself at reception and asked for a double room. I thought at the time that the middle-aged receptionist looked rather strangely at me but thought nothing of it. I was given a key and went to the car to bring in the luggage. A porter suddenly appeared and offered to do the job for me.

He showed us to the room - I gave him a half-crown for his troubles.

We then looked around. The room was twin bedded with the beds at either end - that was bad enough, but not unsurmountable - the real objection, however, were the bars on the windows!!

"This isn't on," I said. "We are, after all, on our honeymoon."

I went to reception and asked for another room.

"We haven't any other rooms available, sir," said the same receptionist who had booked us in, again with an odd look.

"But that one has bars on the windows," I said, embarrassment forcing me to overlook the two single beds and their location.

"I know," she said. "It's to discourage burglars. We haven't any other rooms available."

I thought this was rather strange as the hotel certainly didn't appear busy and there were precious few cars in the car park.

I decided to call her bluff.

"OK - well, if that's the case we will not be staying - we are on our honeymoon - we were married yesterday."

I was getting rather annoyed.

"Ah," she said very coolly. "I thought you looked very young!!"

I was sure she was a loyal catholic woman who thought we were out for a dirty weekend and, with the beds as they were, she certainly wasn't going to help with that!!

We left. The final kick in the teeth for me was that I had to pay another half-crown to the porter to get our bags back in the car!!

Whilst our experience at the Yeats Country Club was a bit disappointing we had no problem getting a room in a hotel in the middle of Sligo town - I was deter-

O'Connell Street, Dublin on honeymoon.

mined the same wouldn't happen again and placed our marriage certificate on the reception desk when I requested a room.

Before we left Tubbercurry, we visited the shop which was at one time run by my Nan's family and paid a call on the local doctor - one of her great friends - who had now retired from medical practice.

Doctor Flannery made us very welcome and, despite the fact that we had just enjoyed a "full Irish with two eggs" in the hotel before we checked out, he would not rest until we joined him at breakfast where we were present-ed with perfectly boiled and very tasty - eggs!!

The remainder of our honeymoon was wonderful.

We travelled to the south of Ireland and stayed on the outskirts of Cork where, once they realised we were honeymooning, were we alloted a beautiful suite, flowers were placed in our room and we were treated like roy-alty.

CHAPTER SEVENTEEN

Teaching

WE returned to the Island - to the house we had rented in Falkland Drive, Onchan. It was an elderly double fronted property which we had secured at two pounds ten shillings a week. The couple whose wedding we had attended the previous year were looking for accommodation and we had the brainwave of sub-letting the top floor of our property.

The landlord had no objections and so, with a little bit of manoeuvring and alteration, we managed to get our own rent down to ten bob a week! Nice work - everyone happy!

We had only been back from honeymoon around six weeks when that euphoria evaporated very quickly. Nana passed away - she had reached the grand age of eighty-eight. She had been bedridden for a year and probably her passing could be considered a blessing, but that didn't lessen the sadness that enveloped us. We were so glad that she had seen her eldest grandson's bride in her wedding dress and that we had been able to visit some friends of her younger life whilst we were on our honeymoon and then report their messages back to her.

One other bit of bad news was that Colin "Shortie" Shaw decided that after his wedding to Margaret the following year, they were going to the UK. Shortie wanted to get some experience in larger firms and we all understood his motives. Little did we all know that this would pre-empt an even bigger move - emigration to New Zealand the year after.

By this time, Flash, Mitch, Shortie and myself had all completed our apprenticeships and there had been a new intake of junior apprentices to take our places. Ffinlo Crellin, Geoff Joughin and Kevin Kelly had joined the company. This threesome in Douglas was complemented by Crawford MacClaren who became junior at *Ramsey Courier*. My brother Nick had decided that he too saw a future for himself in the printing industry. He was taken on as an apprentice machine minder by Herbert Quayle in 1963. Similar to my own aspirations four years hence, they all were keen to learn and to gain as much knowledge of the trade as possible.

NOTHING had changed at the local College of Further Education - the renamed College of Art. Apart from what they could glean from books and have passed on to them by their colleagues, in the circumstances then prevailing the new apprentices were not going to get any proper instruction.

My recently gained qualifications, I had established, were sufficient to enable me to teach the various aspects of the industry. It was worth a try to see if the College would support a move to establish regular classes. Ken Roberts was the new Principal and, after gaining some initial encouragement from Norman Sayle, I met with Ken to discuss the situation. Ken, whilst fully supportive of the proposal, advised me that he had no funds available for the next three months.

"If you are going to do it," he said, "it will have to be an unpaid arrangement until I can get some funds together, but I will support it as much as I can, and when I can I will provide you with some space in the evenings."

There was some very elementary equipment - wooden type, frames, two or three cases of type, paper, ink, etc. - at the College lying unused. I managed to scrounge some more type from the *Ramsey Courier* and Herbert Quayle donated some type, spacing material and some additional kit. One of the local printing firms, hearing of the efforts donated an old Albion press - it was as old and antiquated as could be, but it did operate using the correct principle, so it was welcome.

We began with the theory classes taking place in our home in Laxey one night each week. The four lads from the *Times* office were joined by three or four guys from other firms at times, but the only really keen people were the *Times* apprentices. As well as the theory class, we held a "practical" class each Saturday morning in a basement at Kensington Road.

Ken Roberts was as good as his word and when the three months were up he advised me that I would be able to claim some regular pay as an instructor and we could switch to the College for our theory classes. We were off! The classes went on for three years without a problem - always with the *Times* guys as the regulars - and they were able to sit their relevant City and Guilds examinations as a result. Ken Roberts, Norman Sayle and I all felt that the exercise was a success and very worthwhile. It's a shame the arrangement lasted such a short time, but the advances made in the industry in just those three years meant that a further investment would be substantial if the standard was to be maintained and the attendances just did not warrant the investment.

BACK in the *Times* Office, the publications continued and a new title suddenly appeared: *Babyworld*. As the title suggests, the magazine was directed at pregnant mothers and mothers with new-born babies. It was a brand-new launch by Herbert Quayle's London colleagues and a young blonde called Hilary was sent over as the Editor.

Obviously Hilary attracted a lot of attention from the young male staff in the office but she soon made it apparent that her interests lay only in her editorial responsibilities. We responded by assuming that she was a London "snob" and her attractiveness declined.

After a relatively short period Hilary either moved on of her own accord or she was moved on by her bosses and her replacement arrived. Valerie Roach was a young, very attractive brunette fresh out of university and anxious to make a name for herself in the publishing world. Valerie was as friendly as her predecessor was distant.

I had moved on to the page make-up of *Babyworld* and working with Valerie was a pleasure. She was happy to listen to advice about the technical aspects of producing the magazine whilst, quite rightly, remaining very firm about her editorial ideas and principles. We got on well.

Every Christmas the company organised a Christmas Party, usually held in one of the Promenade hotels where there was plenty of room. One in particular was very successful and held at the Metropole Hotel. Everyone had had a lot to drink and someone suggested that as a break from the dancing, we should have a "Hairy Man" competition.

Amazingly - probably buoyed up by alcohol - Herbert Quayle jumped up, took off his shirt and went to stand alone on the dance floor as the first competitor. Admittedly, he looked quite comical standing bare-chested in the centre of the dance floor - and he was hairy!

Monica, his wife was mortified.

"Herbert, you are the Managing Director," she said. "You can't do that - don't you have any dignity?"

Dignity or not, Herbert was in the competition. The trouble was that when the others realised how hairy he actually was, they decided they could never win anyway and so he became the only entrant.

Monica remained highly miffed and I bet Herbert got it in the neck when they got home that night!

A YOUNG Eunice Salmond had joined the newspaper as a feature writer. She took on the pen name of "Fenella" and had her own column in the paper which rather quickly became the society column for the Island. She was another who was keen to learn the technical side of newspaper production and she thus spent quite a lot of time in the composing room.

Terry Cringle was a new face to me. I had heard of this guy from some of the other reporters and he had returned to the Island after a stint on UK newspapers. He and Allan Bell - the son of previous editor, Billy Bell - became the "stars" of the editorial team and much later went into business together in an agency supplying the UK with Manx news.

CHAPTER EIGHTEEN

Back to the Village

GWYNNETH was pregnant! It must have been the Irish air! Our parents were delighted and so were we, even though it meant that we would have barely ten months together before we became a family.

Gwynneth was not best pleased as she was ill every day and had to give up work much earlier than she had planned. We both felt, however, that the property in Falkland Drive was not ideal for a family and we looked for an alternative.

An opportunity arose for the two of us to secure a rented property on Port-e-Chee Avenue. It was a semi-detached three-bedroomed home which was part of the Douglas Trust and which would be ideal for the three of us. The rent was two pounds ten shillings a week and so we moved.

Gwynneth's Dad helped us buy our car - we had an elderly Austin followed by this equally elderly Vauxhall Wyvern.

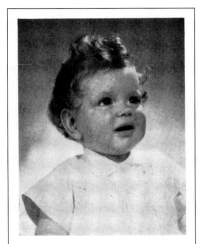

SNAPPED shortly after her first birthday, in one of her rare angelic moments, is 18-month-old Tracey Brown, who hails from Laxey, in the Isle of Man. She has fair, curly hair and brown eyes, and, according to her mother, Mrs. Gwynneth Brown, Tracey is at her happiest when "helping" Mum with her two-month-old sister.

Valerie Roach placed the above entry into one of the early issues of "Babyworld" magazine which she was editing. The "angelic moments" referred to were few and far between!

We needed to make some basic alterations to make the place more comfortable and I knocked down a couple of walls and we installed a new gas fire. It was good, even though our new rent was five times our net commitment in Falkland Drive!

Our baby daughter arrived in June 1963 - almost ten months to the day after our honeymoon! We decided to call her Tracey - she was lovely and we were very proud.

It was very difficult negotiating the steps up to the house from the road - and there were few more, plus an awkward turn, to get in through the front door. The house was certainly not built to accommodate a family with a large pram. Other than that, though, it was a lovely home in which to start out family life.

Gwynneth's Dad was very supportive and he offered to fund the purchase of a car for us which we would repay to him at regular intervals. We first got a small Austin Seven which was never very reliable and then a Vauxhall Wyvern with bench front seats. It was a great car and served us for a number of years.

We had spent some two years at Port-e-Chee during which time I had developed a very good relationship with Gwynn's Dad to the point where he would not go fishing without me.

Edwin had a eighteen-foot inboard motor boat - an ex-lifeboat from a passenger vessel. It was very seaworthy and ideal for all sorts of net fishing - trammel and trawl - lobster fishing, long lines and rod and line. He kept both the boat and his equipment in very good condition and had it moored in Laxey from May to October. Edwin was skilled at net-making and repair and constructed all his own lobster pots from local birch branches and discarded wood. He was never happier than when he was mending his nets in the back yard and I would marvel and the speed he at which he would work.

Summer weekends, we would go out in the evening and lay our trammel nets and lobster pots, perhaps drop a long line and maybe do some rod and line fishing. Then the following morning we would be down at the harbour early, get out to the net and lift the lines and the pots. We caught everything - lobsters, crabs, cod, salmon, flatfish, dogfish (which we used for lobster bait) gurnard which Gwynn's Mum would stuff and roast for a great meal, and so on. We had far too much for our own use and so I used to sell live lobster and crab, in particular, to friendly restaurateurs who I got to know quite well. It was quite profitable and helped to pay for our diesel.

'Oakfield' had a glorious view over the bay and harbour at Laxey. Baby Gwynneth and a lively Tracey are not too concerned about it, however!

However, with our home in Douglas I was restricted to times which allowed for the journey to and from home. This didn't always suit Edwin as he too had to contend with awkward hours especially when he had to go to another port.

So he came up with another offer for us . . .

"I don't believe in renting," he said to me one day. "The property is never your own and you are giving a lot of money each week to somebody else. How about if I lend you the deposit for a house of your own?

I was immediately interested.

"The only thing is . . ."

And I thought - ah, ah.

"I will only do it if you buy a house in Laxey so that Gwynneth can be near her Mum"

Well, that did not present a problem as the thought crossed my mind that it would mean that babysitters were more readily available and we both had a fondness for Laxey anyway.

So the deal was done and we set about looking for a place. One of the first we viewed was the former home of the Kinrade family on Old Laxey Hill. "Oakfield" was an elderly semi-detached double-fronted property with a small front garden and a wonderful view over the harbour. The only drawback was that it still had an outside "loo" - a common feature in many old properties at the time.

We weren't averse to a short walk in the yard, and so we bought it - for £1800 which was funded by Edwin's loan of £200 and an Isle of Man Government loan under their first-time buyers' scheme!

CHAPTER NINETEEN

Challenge for the Chapel

B Y NOW, I had been a journeyman for three years and had become interested in the workings of the Typographical Association. In those days the trade union was a great influence over the printing industry. In London, and in most of the large conurbations, the union ran the industry, especially in the newspaper trade, and it was only years later that the various rackets were exposed which showed how ridiculous the situation had become, especially in Fleet Street.

The original reason for the formation of all unions was to look after their members and to make sure that unscrupulous employers did not take advantage of unsuspecting skilled craftsmen by imposing bad conditions and unduly long hours. The unions also were intended to supply support for families when sickness and ill health kept members away from their work. And finally they were meant to negotiate terms and conditions of employment with employers which were appropriate with the effort put in by the skilled labour of their members.

In the Isle of Man, whilst the union was important within the industry, it never reached a level where it was the primary part of the industry. Employers respected their employees' rights to be a member and, in most instances, they operated their companies within the generally accepted guidelines laid down nationally and accepted by both management and staff.

Looking back, it is my view that H L Dor wanted to be the Eddie Shah of the Isle of Man - it can be recalled that at a later date Eddie Shah launched a completely new UK national newspaper using non-union labour and led the move to vacate Fleet Street and all its "trade union trappings".

The *Times* Office had operated for years paying the staff a rate of pay which was agreed years previously by the *Isle of Man Times* management. The pay equated to a level of pay in the UK called the "Evening News Rate". It had been negotiated nationally as a rate to cover the publication of a daily newspaper which, until recently, the *Isle of Man Times* produced.

As he had ceased the publication of the Wednesday edition - HL announced that the evening news rate of pay would stop and that all staff would be placed on pay equating to the Weekly News Rate. The weekly rate was considerably less and represented quite a drop in pay to every member of the staff.

I had been elected Father of the Chapel following the retirement of Harry Christian. Why I had allowed my name to go forward I will never know, but I did, and now there was a problem, a big problem.

Tommy Jennings, my deputy, and myself called a chapel meeting in the machine room. We stood on the boards of the Miehle press so that we got a bit of height above the assembled staff.

The news had already leaked out but we had to report formally to the meeting: "We have been notified by the management that as from next week, the evening news rate will cease and will be replaced by the weekly newspaper rate", Tommy and I announced.

There was a lot of murmuring and obvious dissension.

"How much will this mean we will lose in our wages," said one member of staff.

We explained the difference between the two rates.

"Disgusting - how will we be able to manage?"

"What can we do?"

"Can we call in the Branch and Head Office?"

The questions came thick and fast. Tommy and I dealt with those we could handle and offered opinions on those which were not within our remit to answer. We did, however, make the point which had been made already to us by the union Head Office that, unfortunately, as HL had in fact closed the Wednesday edition, those editions remaining did not qualify for the evening news rate as there were now only five newspaper editions over a six-day week. The remaining editions were the *Daily Times* on Mondays and Tuesdays, the *Examiner* on Thursdays, the *Weekly Times* on Fridays and the *Green Final* on Saturdays

This essential point was not acceptable to the chapel and they were adamant that the company were out of order in any wage reduction.

"We should "down tools"," came one suggestion.

"Yes, we don't have to accept it," said another.

Tommy and I saw where the meeting was heading. We decided to ask for a show of hands supporting the motion to "down tools" if the management went ahead with the proposal.

The motion was carried unanimously and we were then directed by the chapel to inform the management.

Prior to doing so, Tommy and I thought it prudent to make sure that Head Office was aware of what was about to happen.

"There may be a problem in the union backing such action," they said. "We have already advised that the management's move does not actually break any National Agreement."

Bloody hell! We were on our own and there could be a really serious problem if the action went ahead.

With a degree of trepidation, Tommy and I asked for a meeting with Herbert Quayle.

"Hi, fellas. What can I do for you?" he said, in my opinion, knowing full well what we were there for, as rumours spread like wildfire in a newspaper office.

"We have to advise you, Mr Quayle," I said very carefully, "that if the management go ahead with their stated intention to replace the evening news rate with a weekly rate, the chapel will "down tools"."

Herbert stared at us for a short time, then thumped his desk so hard that his desk calendar jumped in the air.

"Bloody hell," he shouted, "have those buggers no sense whatsoever? How many of them could find themselves out of work as a result of this? Has this been explained to them?"

We assured him that we had tried hard to cover all aspects of the chapel's intended action and the implications it presented.

"Listen," said Herbert, "I know you two are only the message boys, but go back to those buggers and tell them that if they do go on strike - 'cos that's what they are really saying - ten staff will lose their jobs immediately."

We left the office.

"What now?" said Tommy. "We've already explained all the technicalities of the edition's closure to them."

"I know, but now they are going to have to hear it from the "horse's mouth" so to speak, as well as hear Head Office's view on it and the threatened consequences of their actions."

We called another meeting.

Tommy and I relayed piece by piece the meeting we had with Herbert Quayle.

"He told us to tell you that if you do "down tools", ten jobs will be lost."

"He can't do that," said someone. "He would be answerable to the union."

"Unfortunately, that isn't so," we reported, and we told them all about the conversation we had had with union Head Office and the fact that, from their point of view, with the reduction in newspaper production, staff employed by the company no longer could be classed as eligible for payment of the "Evening News Rate" and that the management were not breaking any National Agreement.

"So we're on our own then?"

"I'm afraid that is so," I said, "and Tommy and I need to know what your decision is as a result of being given this information."

There was a lot of argument, some getting rather heated, and we began to feel that we were getting nowhere fast.

"Look," Tommy said, "it's a simple matter - you need to tell us that we go back to management and tell them either that you still intend to "down tools", or you withdraw the threat and accept the reduction."

More argument.

Then a clear voice said, "I can't afford to take the risk."

Another followed, "Neither can I."

But nobody was prepared to propose a motion either way. We had to get a decision, so in the end Tommy and I decided we would propose a motion ourselves and put it to a vote. We went into a huddle to arrange how we could settle it.

Eventually, Tommy proposed a motion that the threat to "down tools" be withdrawn in the light of the management's threats and that further discussions with the management be entered into - I seconded.

I then proposed an amendment to Tommy's motion: that the threat to "down tools" be carried out despite the management's threats - Tommy seconded.

It was all highly irregular as far as voting procedures went but we needed to get a clear mandate and what was the alternative?

My amendment was the first to be put to the meeting - it was unanimously rejected! This meant that Tommy's original motion was bound to be accepted and it was - again unanimously!!

The amazing part to us was that both the amendment and the original motion had been voted unanimously - after all the bickering that had gone on.

I swear to this day that Herbert Quayle somehow knew exactly what had happened at the meeting. What other reason would he have when, at our subsequent meeting, he again mentioned that he saw us as messengers, thanked us for the work we had done and readily agreed to meet with us over the reductions?

Eventually, we managed to reduce the amount of wages which were to be lost which helped and everyone was a little more relieved - except Tommy and I who felt rather foolish in the eyes of the management and bamboozled by our colleagues in the chapel!

CHAPTER TWENTY

Moving On

NEIL Clarke was under great pressure working on *Farmers Weekly* virtually on his own. Lack of monotype experience meant that most members of staff could not help out and Neil was visibly wilting under the strain. Sensibly a decision was made to employ at least one other person with monotype experience to help him and Peter Busby filled the vacancy.

Peter arrived on the Island from the south of England with little or no experience of the Manx way of life, and he found it difficult to come to terms with the changes that needed to be made. I suspect that he played on it at times, but there was often a discussion which ended with Peter being advised that there was "a boat to Liverpool every morning".

He was married to Janet and Gwynneth and I became good friends. Peter smoked a pipe which, frankly, most people couldn't stand, and I think he knew it, but the devil in him kept him smoking. He loved a good argument and delighted in making a statement and then sitting back while others argued the point. In later life Peter became a proof reader and a very good one at that.

AT home, I came to the conclusion that I only had to look at Gwynneth for her to become pregnant!

Gwynneth Jr, our second girl, was born in 1964. She arrived rather swiftly and I was completely unaware until after the event.

It was a Saturday morning and I was teaching. Gwynneth tried to contact me by ringing the College office but, as it was a weekend, it was closed. After the class had finished, I went in to the *Times* Office as I was scheduled for the *Green Final* that weekend.

In Laxey, Gwynneth's family began to worry when I couldn't be contacted and her Dad decided that he wasn't going to take any chances - he packed her into his car and drove her to the maternity home. It was quite a close call as the baby was born some ninety minutes after she arrived. It was all over by the time I found out about it!

THE business of the "down tools" incident had upset and unnerved me. Whilst I appreciated the circumstances and the reason for the change of mind, I couldn't understand how a body of men could be so supportive of their representatives one minute and yet be so ready to unanimously back down the next. It made me question whether or not I was the right man to be the Father of the Chapel and I decided that I was not - I stood down.

At the same time I decided that, much as I was in debt to Herbert Quayle for ensuring I had proper training, I needed a change of environment. An advertisement appeared in the newspaper for someone to join the Tourist Board with a responsibility for ensuring that all printed matter used by the Board for advertising and promotion was properly produced. I really fancied this as it offered some graphic design and estimating experience as well as the technical printing aspect.

I applied and was called for interview by the Chairman of the Tourist Board at the time - I think it may have been a Mr Qualtrough - and Len Bond, who was the Director of Tourism.

The interview was OK until I was questioned on my schooling and asked why I didn't attend King William's College. I told them why and it didn't seem to go down well. I was asked if I was a member of a golf club, had I ever sat on a committee or been a captain? It became apparent that they sought a different type of person - I didn't fit the bill and was unsuccessful.

IT made me even more sure, however, that I needed experience in other companies and other work and so, when a vacancy was advertised in Norris Modern Press, I applied for the job and got it.

The company was small and was basically a stationers. It had been founded originally by Samuel Norris who was an elder statesman of the Island and well-known for his forthright views and political stances. The company generally produced small printed matter but they also produced the *Douglas Weekly Diary* which, essentially, was a small bulletin which advertised forthcoming events mainly for the benefit of the tourists.

The premises were in lower Victoria Street with the printing works located on three floors behind their retail shop.

The whole of the lower portion of Victoria Street and, for that matter, a large part of Loch Promenade is built on shingle which meant that any high tide at that time caused flooding in the basement of any property in these areas.

In Norris's, although they had partitioned the walls and installed a pump to try to cope with the problem, duckboards still had to be used in the basement machine room when the floor was awash with sea water. With the three phase electricity feeds required for the machines, I wonder what today's "elf 'n safety" would have made of that?

I know the same situation existed at the extensive Villiers Hotel which was on the corner of Victoria Street and Loch Promenade and was considered to be one of the prime hotels on the Island. Donald Slee, the manager for many years, decided to turn his basement into a Grill Room and, often in the middle of dinner, one could hear the pumps coming on when the tide was rising!!

My boss at Norris's was Roy Pemberton - a quiet man from the south of the Island. Roy had worked at Norris's for years and had rather fixed views on the owner, Mrs Norris, and her son, Peter. Peter, actually made me very welcome and was always very amiable - his mother was rather different, however.

It was approaching my first Christmas away from the *Times* office where we had been used to an annual party and a small Christmas bonus. Norris's was very busy with corporate Christmas cards, calendars and all things associated with the season. On Christmas Eve, Mrs Norris arrived. We all gathered around the "stone", a central working area in the composing room, and she proceeded to pour us each a sherry.

"Happy Christmas, everyone", she said, had a brief chat with everyone and she left - and that was it!

Roy grinned, "It's been like that ever since I came here." I was taken aback and it brought home how relatively well staff at the newspaper office were treated at Christmas.

Other than that, however, Norris's was a happy shop. I enjoyed my time there and got to know some characters: Doug Davidson, already becoming well-known as he played in his father's dance band, operated one of the machines, Dennis Kneale worked with me as a compositor and his brother Frank worked in the machine room. I recall Cyril Stoutt was the linotype operator - a rather abrasive character who often found himself at odds with Roy Pemberton.

We repaired to the "Dog's Home" for our own Christmas drink: left to right - John Jones, Colin Maxwell, Alan Maddrell, my brother (quite how he is involved I do not know!), me, Doug Davidson and Dennis Kneale.

WE were very happy in our home on Old Laxey Hill - I glanced at Gwynneth again and she announced she was pregnant with our third. It added to the enjoyment - this time we really hoped it would be a boy mainly, for her Dad's sake as we knew he dearly hoped for a grandson.

CHAPTER TWENTY-ONE

Loss of a Friend

EDWIN had become a good friend and I was managing to fit in my fishing with him without a great problem. On occasion, though, I would not be able to get down to the harbour of an evening in time to go out and haul the lobster pots which we usually set along the cliffs north of the harbour.

It wasn't a good idea to leave pots unattended for too long - they could be ruined by an enthusiastic lobster trying hard to escape, the floats could be sheared off by passing vessels, etc., and this meant that, occasionally, Edwin would attend to the pots on his own.

That situation ended, however, when the screw of Edwin's boat fouled one of the pot ropes when he was hauling the pots one evening. Edwin tried hard to free the screw but was conscious of the boat drifting north in the tide. He resorted to rowing the boat back to the harbour and that was no mean task when you were dealing with an eighteen foot vessel with a heavy diesel. He was completely done in when he got back to safety and vowed he would never again go to sea on his own.

Whether the incident had an effect on Edwin's health we will never know, but he became very ill shortly afterwards and, very sadly, never recovered. He was only sixty-two and although past normal retirement age for the Harbour Board, had agreed to work an extra couple of years for them as they were short of Harbourmasters. The poor guy never saw retirement and didn't live long enough to see the birth of his grandson . . . Steven was born only two weeks after Edwin passed away.

Edwin had served in WW2 as a Second Officer in the Isle of Man Steam Packet Company's fleet, which had been commandeered for war operations. Steam Packet vessels were directed to assist in the evacuation at Dunkirk and the *Mona's Queen*, Edwin's ship, was at the forefront of operations. She struck a mine outside the harbour and sank very quickly. The only survivors of the blast all gathered in one lifeboat and, fortunately, were picked up. For Edwin, it was extremely fortunate as he had never learned to swim!!

Edwin Cregeen, third from the right front row behind the lifebelt, pictured with his fellow officers and crew of the ill-fated "Mona's Queen" which struck a mine off Dunkirk during the evacuation of the second world war. This image is featured in the Manx National Heritage's excellent House of Mannanan at Peel and is part of the Ted Groom Collection.

Many years later, Gwynneth and I paid a visit to the recently opened House of Mannannan at Peel. We reached the top floor which had been dedicated to the part the Isle of Man Steam Packet Company had played in the history of the Island. The area had been fitted out to resemble the bridge of one of the Steam Packet vessels and there were illustrations of the company's history fixed to the walls. We were approaching the end of the display and Gwynneth suddenly turned and came face-to-face with a life-sized photograph of her Dad! What a shock! Edwin had been photographed in a group along with his mates on the deck of the *Mona's Queen*.

Gwynn's Mum, Annie, was alone and living on her own in the property at the foot of Old Laxey Hill which she and Edwin, in preparation for retirement, had bought. Conscious of her dislike for such a situation, we suggested that it may be helpful to her to come and live with us. Annie readily agreed, the property was sold and Annie moved in with us.

MANY of the friends of Gwynneth and I were involved in the tourist business which, in those days, was a great industry to be in as the season normally extended from around the end of April to the end of October. Full-time involvement in the industry meant you worked hard for half the year and then relaxed during the winter, living on the profits made during the season.

We began to think that we would like such an arrangement and started to make enquiries.

Tourist businesses could be run in either rented properties, when a change of ownership concerned the "ingoing" only, or in properties fully owned by the business. There was no way we could afford any tourist properties, but an "ingoing" became available in Stanley Terrace on Broadway and we took the plunge.

Number Seven was a thirteen-bedroomed property with some private accommodation for the owners in a specially constructed attic. It worked well for us as my classes at College didn't operate during the summer months and we had three happy years there producing a nice additional income for the family. Annie also found pleasure in helping out when required, so we all benefitted.

DESPITE the friendliness of the surroundings and staff, I never really settled at Norris's and I was presented with an opportunity to move on by Benny Howland, the union secretary.

Benny sought me out to advise me that he had been approached by the Managing Director of Starline Industries - a production unit of Starline Industries of Blackpool - which had recently been set up at Peel. Benny had been asked if he knew of anyone who would be keen to take on the role of composing room foreman in the company.

I met with the Managing Director, Ron Peacham, and although I was not crazy over the financial offer he made to me, I decided that the experience gained would compensate and so joined the company.

Normally the first few days in any new employment often set the scene for the future as far as an employee's view of his new company is concerned - they usually make you decide whether or not you have made the right decision.

In this instance, I couldn't make up my mind. Along with most of my colleagues, I was driven to Peel and back each day by the Managing Director as we all were Douglas residents. This process, whilst economic for the employees, was rather boring and, if there had been some discontent during the day as sometimes was the case, the atmosphere during the drive could be tense to say the least.

The printing facility was located in what was the disused Peel Clothworkers' Primary School which, with the building of a replacement school further up the road, had become vacant. The building was far from ideal for a printing works - the various rooms were much too small and the whole set-up portrayed an amateurish air.

The work carried out by the company mainly consisted of the supply of calendars, diaries and business gifts to the head office of the operation in Blackpool. The system was that at the beginning of each year, calendars for the forthcoming year were printed leaving space on each page for an over-printed personalisation to be carried out later in the year. The same system applied to diaries.

Starline's head office band of sales representatives then went around the UK selling both calendars and diaries to companies who subsequently used them for Christmas gifts and the like. The reps were not paid a salary by Starline, but they received substantial commission on each calendar or diary sold and their income each year could, as a result, be quite high.

It was quite a good system which seemed to keep us busy most of the time either producing the bulk stock or overprinting for specific customers, but it was somewhat boring and the problem was that there was very little alternative work coming in despite the fact that Peacham had, apparently, been given a brief to seek local business as well.

Each company has its own characters and Starline was no different. Peacham, himself was an enigmatic man - he managed to make himself scarce very often, always having a lucid reason for his absence. From my point of view, that didn't matter too much as I wasn't particularly keen on the man and was quite happy to work on in his absence. Philip Parker, my composing room colleague, who was quite an astute person, had a similar view of 'our boss' to myself.

The machine room was staffed by Bill Wade and Arthur Quilliam. Arthur had been an apprentice in the *Times* Office whilst I was there and I therefore knew him quite well. Bill was a young and very quiet machine oper-ator who later moved on to spend a long time with Bridson and Horrox in Douglas and then moved to the south of England. Interestingly, a few years ago Bill's son, John, joined the Mannin Media staff at Tromode.

A regular visitor to the premises was Mike Buchanan. Mike was retained by Starline in Blackpool as their representative on the Isle of Man and often popped in to see how his orders were progressing. We suggested to Mike that he should try to get us some general printing work whilst he was visiting his clients. I think Mike genuinely tried to do so but he was never encouraged in this direction by Ron Peacham and he lost interest.

Head Office organised an awards ceremony and party, usually around Christmas, at which presentations were made to the representatives who had performed particularly well during the previous year. They proved quite riotous occasions - I attended a couple of them!

CHAPTER TWENTY-TWO

B&Hx and the TA

A VACANCY had arisen on the Branch Committee of the union and I was elected. The monthly meetings were held in Benny Howland's front room in Palatine Road and were normally interesting and quite enjoyable. Benny was a dedicated unionist who believed strongly in the basic principles of trade unionism. He often had run-ins with managements, but sometimes seemed more committed to ensuring that members "toed the line."

The Typographical Association was one of the more active and influential movements of the day. As mentioned previously, the union was in charge of Fleet Street and the national newspaper bosses had to jump through hoops to satisfy the officials in the various printing plants. Other than a couple of other cities - Liverpool in particular - throughout the rest of the UK, the union performed firmly but sensibly.

It was well organised with a General President, a National Council and various Head Office representatives all of whom had been elected to their posts by the membership. The union was divided into areas each with their own Head Office representation. Areas, individually, held an Annual Conference and there was a Bi-annual Conference of the whole union to which representatives of each branch were sent.

It was during this period that I had my first experience of representing the Isle of Man Branch at Conference when the Branch selected me to attend the North-West Area Annual Conference in Liverpool. The conference was on a Saturday and I flew to Liverpool the night before. I hadn't a clue what to expect, but was impressed with the organisation which had gone into the event and the manner with which it was being run by a Chairman with obvious wide experience. He needed it at times, especially when certain representatives from the Liverpool Branch took the floor. These guys attacked employers with venom and one couldn't help feeling that it was their desire to see the whole industry run by the union, never mind Fleet Street.

I reported back to the local branch and sent a report for circulation to the membership.

STARLINE Industries was not for me! I stuck it out for as long as I could but as soon as an opportunity arose for me to move, I grabbed it.

Bridson and Horrox placed an advertisement in the local press for a compositor and I applied for the job. I was interviewed by Ian Horrox, the son of Harry Horrox one of the original founders of the company in the 1930s. Ian was very proud of his company, and rightly so - they were doing very well and certainly were by far the busiest and best of the smaller print operations on the Island. Their premises were in Back Strand Street opposite the present rear entrance to Marks and Spencer and, although it seemed a small place with a single fronted shop on the roadside, Ian had been very astute in property acquisitions nearby, and the overall area used for printing was quite large.

Ian decided I was worth the risk and took me upstairs to meet the composing room foreman, Alan Bell, and Archie Knudsen, Ian's right hand man who had been with the company for many years.

The difference between the operation at B&Hx, as it was commonly referred, and that at Starline was immense. Work piled in to B&Hx at a great rate of knots and it was obvious that the company was doing exceptionally well. How much of that was due to Ian's individual efforts, to Archie's attempts to bring business in or just a feature of the current market, I don't know, but they were certainly busy.

Whilst Ian ran a tight ship, he was an excellent businessman and operated very professionally, his staff were also a major part of the firm's success. There was a total staff of around a dozen at that time and the principals consisted of: Alan Bell, who had joined the company after a move from the UK. Alan was excellent at his job, determined and keen to advance as much as he could in the industry. When I arrived at the company, Ian Ward was just approaching the end of his apprenticeship as a compositor. Ian was a quiet, efficient lad who got on well with everyone. The composing room was later extended by the addition of Roy Wilson who also moved from the UK.

In the machine room, Peter Corrin had served his apprenticeship with the company and was an important part of the production team. Peter was joined later by Liverpudlian, Ian Sommer, who had married Anne, a local girl whose family I knew. The bindery was basically run by Brian Cannell. It was a reflection on the company that, for many of the staff, B&Hx had been their only employer.

I settled in quickly and began to enjoy the work.

AFTER the trials and tribulations of the first few months we had also begun to enjoy running the boarding house and had learned many of the tricks of the trade. We tried hard to serve our guests with the freshest possible produce and to vary the food as much as possible. This meant, perhaps, that we had to spend more time in the kitchen, but we felt that our guests appreciated it.

We had found other friends in the business and had established a good relationship with some of the neighbours who, obviously, were also running establishments. Peter and Corrin Ollerenshaw ran a larger property across the road from us and we became good pals.

1970 was our third season and our best yet. We had thoughts of moving on to other, larger premises but the only drawback we found in the whole business of looking after tourists was the embarrassment we experienced when showing them to their room if they were unfortunate in being placed in a rear bedroom where the view consisted of a blank wall. As most of the larger premises were on the Promenade or in the Drives and had very few rooms at the front of the property, it was difficult to find anywhere which did not have this problem.

There was also no doubt that the tourism business for the Island was beginning to reduce. The vast numbers who holidayed here in the early 1960s were beginning to be more selective in their requirements and sought the sun. They began to ask for en-suite facilities and were not prepared to share toilets and bathroom facilities with the other people on their landing.

We were undecided what we should do, but then, I looked at Gwynneth again - she was pregnant! Our future was decided!

It was obvious that whilst Gwynneth had worked wonders running the place with three young children, a fourth was stretching things to the limit and we both felt we needed to move so she wasn't so tied down with the responsibilities attached to the business.

Gwynn's sister Ann was keen to get back to work and she invited their mother, Annie, to spend some time with her and Eric so that she could be home for Helen, their daughter, when she returned from school. So Annie moved to Farrant Street and we began looking for a new home.

Before too long we found an ideal place in Westminster Drive adjacent to Ballakermeen School. It was in the middle of a terrace of four properties - three bedrooms, bathroom, lounge, parlour and small kitchen with a quite large outhouse which I earmarked for expansion. There was no front garden to speak of, but there was quite a long patch at the rear which would be ideal for vegetables. Best of all, it was not expensive as the previous owners recognised that there was work needed to bring the home up to scratch.

We sold the ingoing of Stanley Terrace quite swiftly - maybe too swiftly and too cheaply - but we were able to secure a mortgage on Westminster Drive at a good rate and we moved early in 1971. We immediately set about the alterations which we knew were needed - we knocked a wall down, extended the kitchen into the outhouse and decorated from top to bottom. Before too long we had a lovely home.

Sarah was born in April 1971 - we had been married less than nine years, had four children and had lived in five different homes - quite an achievement!

Tracey and Gwynneth Jr were already attending Murrays Road junior school and it was time for Steven to start his education. Gwynneth arranged for him to attend Ballaquayle primary in Stoney Road and took him there after Easter for the first time. Apparently, after a short while, Steven decided he didn't like it and wanted to go home so he up and left. The school caretaker caught up with him marching home in Albany Road and brought him back to the school. After that incident, the school gates were kept firmly closed during classes.

Nick had completed his apprenticeship at the *Times* Office and decided he wanted to widen his experience in the trade. He felt, probably correctly, that the only way to ensure this was to move to the UK to a much larger print operation, so he applied for and was given a job with Tinlings, a very large book and journal printing company in Liverpool. He remained there for a year, but the pull of the Island became too much and he returned to work again at the *Times* Office.

The Brown family at Nick and May's wedding. From the left - back row: Uncle Billy McKibbin, Uncle Tom Quayle, Joan McKibbin, Norman McKibbin (cousin). Second row: Gwynneth, Auntie Flo (K Michael), Auntie Muriel, Auntie Ethel, Auntie Myra, Auntie Flo, Auntie Freda. Front row: John, Mum, Nick, May, myself, Gordon Malcolm. Page boy: Steven. Bridesmaids: Tracey and Gwynneth.

He had been engaged to May Callister, whom he had met whilst they both were employed in the *Times* office for some time and they were married in 1971 at Laxey with a lovely reception at the Queens Hotel in Ramsey. After their honeymoon they lived in Mount Havelock, Douglas and eventually bought a property in Onchan.

IT WAS around this time that H L Dor decided that he would separate the newspapers from the general printing and he moved all of the newspaper production and editorial staff to Hill Street - the old premises of the *Isle of Man Examiner*.

The general printing department remained *in situ* at the *Times* Office and HL brought in his stepson, Michael Devitt, to run the operation which was renamed the Island Development Company Limited and then renamed again: Mannin Printers.

SHORTLY after I began work at B&Hx, Benny Howland decided to stand down as Branch Secretary of the union. Though I had some doubts about it, I allowed my name to go forward for nomination and was elected unopposed.

Fred Wharton, the ex-Liverpool Branch Secretary, had also stood down from his union work in Liverpool and he headed up a typesetting company which he brought to the Island and set up shop in School Road, Onchan. Keyspools Limited were not printers - they typeset on monotype machines producing punched tape which was then sent to the UK to be converted into pages for books.

Fred had brought about six staff with him including Roy Livermore who seemed to be the senior. Roy had joined the Branch Committee and he was elected President to serve with me.

Roy and I got on very well - it was a good combination as Roy had a lot more experience than me in trade union work and I knew the local scene better than he did, so we worked well together. I greatly valued his advice which, at times, was sorely needed and Erica, Roy's wife, became good friends with Gwynneth. It was a "happy marriage" all round.

Roy and I attended a number of conferences together. One, in particular, was in Harrogate when Joe Cannell was part of the Isle of Man delegation and the Isle of Man Branch had put down a motion for consideration at the conference. The normal procedure was for the Branch representatives to move and second any motion their Branch had proposed. This meant a speech to around 1500 delegates . . . I was scared stiff!

I stood in the queue of speakers just below the rostrum waiting my turn to be called by the President, Fred Simmons, who was in the chair. The guy in front of me was proposing a motion very similar to ours. He, too, was very nervous and when he finished and came down the two or three steps to

Joe Cannell, one of the first journeymen I met when I commenced my apprenticeship. Joe originally was a linotype operator who, when phototypesetting was introduced to the Manx industry in the mid-1970s, retrained to successfully operate a computer typesetter for many years. Joe was also a valiant member of the committee of the local branch of the NGA, serving as President and Secretary and his support and advice was greatly valued. He was also an excellent footballer for St. Georges.

the conference floor, he whispered that he was glad it was over . . . wonderful! Just what I wanted to hear!

I stood on the first step of the rostrum and kindly Fred announced, "Ladies and gentlemen, if the delegate from the Isle of Man agrees, conference will be happy to amalgamate the Isle of Man motion with the previous motion so there will be no need for a proposal."

I quickly nodded the Isle of Man's approval and scarpered! Good old Fred!

On another occasion Roy and I were called to an emergency meeting of the union in London. National wages negotiations had broken down. A general strike within the industry was brewing and the union were making preparations to ensure that it would be successful. The conference hall was packed. We sought out some guys we knew from the north west area and we all sat and listened whilst the arrangements were decided. An attempt to hijack the conference and force more militant action was made by the idiots from Liverpool but they were put down very efficiently by the union hierarchy.

After the conference was over most delegates returned to their branches the same evening but we had to wait until he following morning for the train to Liverpool and the boat home. We decided we would have a night out and the other guys we had met joined us. All five of us went to Raymond's Revue Bar in Soho. We had a good laugh but I doubt if I have ever paid so much for a bottle of beer, nor made it last so long!

When we got back to the Island, we had to call an emergency Branch meeting to report on what was about to happen. It was serious and a strike, if it materialised, could well be long-running. At the very least, there would be a ban on all overtime and a work-to-rule imposed. The members were worried, we all were, and Roy and I were at the forefront of it.

We organised the meeting in the Auto Club in Hill Street. When it concluded I came out of the meeting, and heard my name called. I realised that it was coming from a parked car and found it was Ian Horrox waiting for me. Ian knew the meeting was serious and that the industry in the Island could be hit hard.

"Hop in," said Ian, "I'll give you a lift home."

"What's the decision, then?" he said, after a short while.

"I can't discuss it with you, Ian. It's a matter for the Branch and you will know soon enough."

I was quite taken aback that he should expect me to discuss the matter with him - but it got worse . . .

"Well, if there is a strike," said Ian, "it won't affect B&Hx too much will it? After all, you do work there!"

Ian was, quite naturally, worried about the effect industrial action would have on the company. That concern was also felt by the union members, but obviously every office had to be treated the same.

"Look, Ian, if there is a strike, it will affect every unionised

Roy Livermore was President of the Isle of Man Branch of the National Graphical Association which was the new name for the old Typographical Association. With Roy's support, I attended many meetings and conferences in the UK on behalf of the local branch. In our later working lives, we worked together in Mannin Media. As with Joe Cannell, I was appreciative of his advice and it was a blow to the Manx printing industry when at a relatively early age, Roy suddenly passed away a few years ago.

printing company in the Island. There will be no exceptions. The issue is national - it's not in the hands of the local branch to make decisions affecting individual offices."

Ian was not pleased and the remainder of the drive was subjected to a rather strained silence.

I expected relationships to be rather strained the next morning as well but no, it was as if the incident had never occurred, and the matter was never raised again!

As it happened, although I did not report it to Ian, the previous night there had been a proposal put forward that if there was to be a strike Roy and I would seek exemption for the Island, based upon the insignificant effect it would have on the UK situation.

There was a general strike - the Isle of Man was declared exempt and, instead, on the Island there was a ban on all overtime and a work to rule both of which were extremely difficult for Roy and I to enforce.

CHAPTER TWENTY-THREE

"Lemon on your Chicken, Sir?"

THE AMOUNT of work coming in to B&Hx was colossal. It covered all aspects of printing and ranged from small quantities of business cards to large books sometimes requiring quite big quantities.

Big profit earners for the company were the Annual Reports and Accounts which many companies were legally bound to produce each year. The large profit they created was generally due to the indecision of the accountants and finance guys when the time came to sign off and print. "Author's corrections" to work which had already been typeset and proofed were a very expensive additional charge and boosted the turnover substantially.

But the big money spinner at that time was the requirement of the Island's emerging company registration sector which was being greatly promoted and assisted by the Government of the day.

The Isle of Man Government had woken up to the differential between tax imposed in the UK and the tax regime they had on the Island. The difference was substantial and that, a combination of other attractive financial incentives, along with the fact that there were no death duties, made the Island a very interesting prospect for business.

However, in the main it was necessary to be seen to be actively involved in business on the Island in order for many of the incentives to apply. This meant there was a sudden explosion in the number of new companies being formed and registered on the Island. Each one had to have, by law, its own Memorandum and Articles of Association which had to be properly printed.

Pure Manna from Heaven for B&Hx!

Memos & Arts, as they became known, consisted in effect of all the activities in which the company was involved, its members - shareholders - and the rules under which it could operate. The whole "booklet" would consist of around sixteen pages of foolscap, stapled at the spine and supplied in quantities of ten. Normally they would be ordered by the lawyers in Athol Street, sometimes by accountants but invariably it was old school colleagues of Ian Horrox, who was an ex-pupil of King Bill's, who sent him the work - the "old school tie" system operating at its most effective.

As most new companies were formed for the same reason - matters of tax - the activities section and other descriptive parts of the "booklet" were identical and the only changes made in many instances would be the company name and the participants - the members. These fell on two of the sixteen pages only and took a matter of minutes to change, but the charge made was such that it covered all sixteen pages as if they had been typeset from scratch each time.

What a winner! Soon there were so many orders that the legal firms began to order the Memos & Arts in blank form in bulk with a name assigned to each, and then sent them back to be finally printed with the names of the participants. It didn't matter - the customers thought that by ordering them in bulk they were saving money. They were receiving a small discount for quantity which is normal business practice, but in fact such an arrangement increased the turnover for B&Hx - they couldn't go wrong.

It was boring work for the staff but great for the overtime and we all knew what a money-spinner it was. Alan Bell had made a number of personal contacts in Athol Street and knew he could secure a few bulk orders himself from them for Memos & Arts and probably at a marginally smaller cost than if the order was placed with the company.

"I'm damned if I'm going to just bring them here for the sole benefit of Ian, though," said Alan. "I'm going to see if he will do a deal with me."

We reckoned he didn't have a chance but anyway he met with Ian and, indeed, struck a deal whereby he paid Ian for the use of his equipment, paid us for working on them and made his own nice profit. The only thing insisted on by Ian was that any work done for Alan did not have any detrimental effect on the company's own work. That wasn't a problem - to us it just meant even more overtime!!

THE North West Area of what had become the National Graphical Association - the union - decided to hold their Annual Conference in the Isle of Man. It was a reasonable-sized conference with around 500 delegates and the actual conference itself was to be centred in the Villa Marina.

One of the main conference hotels was the Villiers and it was here that the local Branch decided to hold their welcome "get-together" on the Friday evening before the conference proper opened the following day. The Branch invited all the main officials from the Area Office and from Head Office along with representatives of the Isle of Man employers, local Fathers of the Chapels and the members of the Branch Committee.

We were rather keen to conserve costs as much as possible and asked Donald Slee, the hotel manager, for menu suggestions. He suggested that, as it was a very informal North West Area affair, chicken and chips in a basket would be most appropriate. We thought it was a great idea.

The evening passed very quickly - we had very short speeches, as everyone was keen to enjoy themselves prior to the serious business of the conference, Roy and myself sat with our wives around a coffee table in the company of Herbert Quayle, who had accepted the invitation on behalf of the local employers, his wife Monica, NGA President Fred Simmons and his wife, the area President and his wife and the Area Organiser Bryn Griffiths. We all had a few drinks but were still relatively sober.

The excellent chicken and chips were served in a rather nice wicker basket along with some sauce in a plastic sachet and within a few minutes I caught Roy's eye. He winked at me and nodded in the direction of Herbert who was in the process of twisting something over his chicken.

"This is a new method of putting lemon juice on your chicken, isn't it?" said Herbert.

Nobody had the nerve to answer - the poor guy had mistaken the hand wipe, scented with lemon, which Donald had supplied for use after the food was eaten, for an additional condiment for the food!

Not a word was said at the time and, to our knowledge, Herbert never realised, but my word it raised many a laugh in later years.

THE work as Branch Secretary gave me almost a free rein to come and go into all the print companies on union business. It was important not to abuse the facility, however, so I always made sure that I requested permission before walking in.

There had been changes made in the arrangements for the newspapers and the *Examiner* building in Hill Street had been brought back into use by H L Dor. His stepson, Michael Devitt had

Herbert Quayle served during the war with the Manx Regiment and cemented his relationship with the Radcliffe family at the time. When HL Dor bought the Isle of Man Examiner business from them, Herbert was already installed as Managing Director. and he became HL's right-hand man for many years, eventually retiring from day-to-day affairs into a position as Company President. Herbert was a very likeable man and always displayed the friendly characteristics which, in my opinion, were not part of HL Dor's make-up. He was extremely loyal as well and I doubt if HL ever fully appreciated his support.

taken over operations in Athol Street and ran it as a general printing company. It had additional facilities for the production of magazines.

Mainly because it contained the largest union membership, there were many issues in the *Examiner* office and I seemed to be in and out of the place two or three times a week.

On one visit, I bumped into Herbert Quayle and in his normal, friendly manner we were chatting about how things were going and what was happening in the industry.

"You're not half spending some time in here," said Herbert. "You may as well come and work here."

"You couldn't afford me," I joked, laughing.

"What are you talking about, man? Come and see me next week - we need to talk."

I thought no more of it until I took a phone call at B&Hx the following week.

"I thought you were coming to see me," said Herbert.

"I thought you were joking,"

"Well, I'm not. Come and see me next Monday - OK?"

The company had decided that they required a Production Manager. I was aware that they had installed a new web-offset press to undertake the production of the newspapers. The web-offset process was relatively new and was much superior to the letterpress process used by the old Cossar press, especially in the reproduction of photographs and illustrations.

Once the web-offset was up and running properly they were going to look at photo-typesetting - again this was a new process which took over from the trusty Linotypes. Both processes required substantial retraining of staff and a properly thought out installation sequence covering the phototypesetting development. It was a big challenge.

Finally, although he was very careful not to be specific, over the next couple of years Herbert was to retire and the company would be looking for a replacement Managing Director.

True to form, the question of salary was not raised until near the end of the interview. Herbert asked what I was being paid at B&Hx. I had anticipated such an enquiry and had worked out my overall salary including the overtime so, after adding on a little bit for luck, I gave him the figure.

"That's not a problem - we can better that."

He did but only by a few pounds a week, however, the challenge was an attractive one and, like the poacher becoming the gamekeeper, I went for it.

Ian Horrox had always been a good employer. When I informed him of the offer from the *Examiner*, he encouraged me to take the job as he saw it as a good opportunity for me to step into management and I left B&Hx with goodwill on both sides.

CHAPTER TWENTY-FOUR

A New Production

S O IT was another life-changing moment! I had switched sides from senior union representative on the Island to a senior management position in the Isle of Man's largest company. I did receive supportive comments from most of my colleagues on the Branch Committee and there were the usual snide remarks one would expect from others, but to my way of thinking, it was a no brainer and if I wanted to advance myself in the industry, it was obvious I had to take it.

There was one nagging doubt - HL Dor. His name had not been raised in the meeting I had with Herbert Quayle. I realised that another meeting was necessary to discuss a number of points, not the least of which was to establish the extent of my responsibilities. We met away from the office where I felt Herbert would be a little more forthcoming.

I asked a lot of very pointed questions. We quickly established that my responsibilities would cover virtually all aspects of production and associated staff with the exception of editorial. I specifically requested this should be excluded as I felt I was not in a position to make decisions in that department. The only rider Herbert added was that if I felt that a person was not good enough and should no longer work for the company, he was to be part of that decision. That was an easy issue with which to agree.

Herbert was, I believe, very honest with his responses, but I could not help but be suspicious that his loyalty prevented him from saying anything which would portray the owner of the company in a poor light. In the main the meeting was encouraging, but I was left still with some doubts over the influence Dor had in the company and whether or not his interference would prove a problem. I resolved to tackle that problem if and when it arose.

The first few days were spent getting to know staff in each department. Most of the printing staff I knew well already. I could relate quickly to them and it was a relatively easy matter to listen to their views and their concerns on what was required in the company. In newspapers, working to a deadline is normal for every department from editorial through typesetting, process and machining. When deadlines are not met the reason, invariably, is the actions, or lack of them, of the previous department - typesetting will blame late copy from editorial, process will blame late final pages from typesetting, and machining will blame late plates from process.

My job as Production Manager was to try to get the whole production operation operating to deadlines. On the print side, that is from the time the copy was received from editorial, deadlines were usually met. It was far from simple to convince editorial, however, that the maintenance of deadlines was equally as important as the news content. The real problem was the amount of pride the editor had in the content of the newspaper. It was entirely under-standable that he or she always wanted their product to be well received and look good. The trouble was that this meant that if a sniff of a story broke fif-teen minutes before deadline, deadline was extended to make sure the story got in the edition. It was a fundamental problem which was never really solved.

Many of the typesetting guys from the *Times* Office had moved to the *Examiner* - Joe Cannell, Bob McFee, Brian Kneen, amongst them. Peter McElroy, later to become an integral part of Mannin Media, joined from the *Ramsey Courier*. Ron Southall, a chronic diabetic, had also joined as a typeset-ter. Ron was quite a character who continually made light of his condition. He was never averse to injecting himself wherever he was, at whatever time of the day he felt he needed it - it used to make my toes curl and I have been conscious of the seriousness of diabetes ever since. Very sadly Ron died very suddenly whilst out shopping in Douglas.

After the typesetting of a story was complete, it had to be prepared for reproduction and was pasted into position on a blank sheet of paper the same size as the eventual newspaper. In order to fit in the columns of type, all of the excess of photographic paper which was used to typeset the story had to be trimmed off, usually with a scalpel and steel rule.. Whenever the deadline appeared to be in danger, I would 'lend a hand' wherever needed and I often trimmed my share of typesetting.

Until a couple of years ago, I have to admit to being a compulsive nail-biter and consequently never had any protection at the end of my fingers. During trimming one afternoon I sliced off a small portion at the end of my left index finger with the scalpel. Of course, as usual, the smaller the cut the larger the bleed and suddenly there was a panic to find the first aid box.

I was as much concerned about a delay to production as I was to my finger, but the blood was flowing quite freely.

"Come on, lads, where's the bloody plasters," I called.

"I'm coming, I'm coming," said Ron Southall who, because of his condition and his membership of St John Ambulance, was the natural con-tender to be the first aid man. "There's no need to panic - that red stuff is not blood anyway, in your case it's printers' ink!"

LES Hewitt was operating the new Pacer web-offset to the best of his ability but it was revealed that his "re-training", rather stupidly, had consisted of a mere few days with the installation engineer when the press was installed. As a result he was having difficulties. Les was supported on the press by Allan Parrock and, at production times, by Giovanni "Johnny" Moneta, a great character who had been interned at Knockaloe during WW2 due to his Italian nationality - he was from the Island of Elba. Many of Les's colleagues from Athol Street had moved on but John Shimmin remained.

I contacted Linotype who were the manufacturers of the Pacer press, explained the situation to them and came to an agreement with them that they would supply a demonstrator for the press for two weeks which, hopefully would help with training.

Jack Sillick was in charge of the process department which made the plates for each page of the newspaper to be clipped on to the units of the Pacer for printing. David Callister was his number two.

It was quite a laborious method of production - especially when compared to today's computerised methods - consisting of photographing the completed page, developing it as a negative, photographically transferring the negative image to a plate and then developing the plate and drying it for the press. Altogether, to produce a plate from a completed page would take around twelve minutes, but when you were behind the deadline, it always seemed to take half an hour.

Jack was a lovely guy but old school. David's age meant he was of the more modern outlook. It was against Jack's principles to rush the making of a plate as it could compromise the quality. David, on the other hand, was more realistic in accepting the need for speed and took the view that any difference in quality was not apparent anyway.

This meant that when the deadline approached, David was invariably my target to produce the plates. Soon Jack began to realise and accept the need for speed and the process department became a much slicker and more efficient operation as a result.

The advertising sales department was under the control of Hadyn Shimmin who was supported by Arthur Scarffe and Doug Faragher, as well as a couple of junior staff. Selling advertisements is never an easy job - you are actually selling a blank space and the only sales aids you can use are price and circulation. In the case of the *Examiner* and its sister papers, decisions made in later months by the owner made selling space even more difficult.

The advertising revenue is always the most important aspect of a newspaper business in terms if its viability and so the level of advertising income is invariably checked every week. During my tenure, however, I received more support from this department to keep to deadlines than I ever did from editorial and I often made that point to anyone who would listen.

The company's Christmas Dinner Dance was invariably an excellent night enjoyed here by Mrs Jill Shimmin, Haydn Shimmin, Mrs Monica Quayle, Herbert Quayle, Gwynneth, myself and Valerie Roach.

Eric Kinrade was now firmly entrenched as Editor and the editorial department was boosted with the appearance of Sydney Boulton. Sydney was a Ramsey man through and through and had worked for many years at the *Ramsey Courier*, latterly as editor. His writing ability was phenomenal and, strongly supported by Robert Kelly who had been part of the team for some time, the standard of reporting and feature writing was very high.

My namesake Colin Brown joined the company! Colin was an excellent journalist who excelled at sport - mainly tennis and table-tennis - and often looked after the sports pages of the paper. I lost count of the number of times I answered the telephone to hear "the results of last Saturday's tennis matches" and had to transfer them upstairs with an explanation. Gwynneth and I have also taken many calls at home which were for Colin or Margaret, his wife, and I'm sure that the situation happened in reverse.

Bit by bit progress in timings for production was made. We leaned heavily on suppliers to give us as much on-site training as possible for their products. As a result we had visits from Howson-Algraphy to demonstrate their plates and chemicals, Gibbons to advise us on inks and so forth.

I met with John Swale who had installed a very similar type of web-offset press at his newspaper offices in Merseyside. John had suffered badly from the interference of the Liverpool trade union branch to the point where he was heartily sick of the whole industry. He was a man of great experience, however, and I knew a lot could be learned from talking regularly to him. I also visited his offices on one occasion when production was proceeding normally - apparently this was rather a rarity as invariably there was a "work to rule" or an "overtime ban" in place.

I began to think of the proposed move to phototypesetting and started making enquiries to suppliers. At the time a firm called Compugraphic was making a name for itself in the field of phototypesetting and I was invited to view their products at their Yorkshire base and at some of the installations they had in Yorkshire, Scotland and in Lancashire.

Their sales representative was Gordon Stirling who lived near Peebles in the border country. Gordon was a young guy, a trained compositor who had turned to sales and who had undergone intensive training on the advantages of Compugraphic's gear. Gordon was a very nice man, far from your usual "pushy" sales representative, and you could see that he was always keen to establish good relationships with his clients by advising them properly. In our case, the fact that we were an Island installation and that servicing the kit was not just a matter of driving down the road for the engineer, was vital.

I looked at the full range of equipment at their Head Office and then Gordon and I visited three installations where I was able talk frankly to the operators and the managers about the advantages and disadvantages of the kit. One of the installations visited was Johnston Press in Falkirk - Fred Johnston was a great person to advise on our situation and I listened to him with great care. His firm has now become one of the largest public companies in the UK, and the owners of Isle of Man Newspapers Limited. Its a funny old world!

After a few months of consideration the *Examiner* decided to buy Compugraphic typesetters linked with Datek keyboards which produced the punched tape used to drive the typesetters. In addition two Compugraphic machines arrived which produced larger sized type for headlines.

The big element in the switch to this type of composition for the typesetting staff was that the keyboards of the Dateks were based upon the QWERTY layout - the same as that used in typewriters and in all modern computers. The staff had been used to the old Linotype keyboards which were completely different. In the UK this was one of the fundamental reasons for opposition, by the trade union, to phototypesetting in many areas. The union felt that it would be the easiest thing in the world to bring in typists, who were more used to the different layout, to operate the new keyboards and skilled men may lose their jobs. They were basically correct; such a move would have been very convenient for a company, but in the end most opted for retraining for their operators.

There was never a large staff in pre-press at the *Examiner* and during holidays, the staff level reduced even further. Most of the retraining was undertaken at the machines by the operators themselves and it was a credit to them that the retraining went as well as it did. During the switch to full phototypesetting the papers were produced using a mixture of photographic proofs from the new phototype system and "galley" proofs from the original Linotypes and the difference could quite easily be seen in the finished product. However, eventually we got there.

CHAPTER TWENTY-FIVE

Disaster Number Two

BY LATE summer 1973, things had begun to settle down and Gwynneth and I decided that it was time we had a family holiday - we had not been off the Island other than on business since our honeymoon eleven years earlier.

Our resources were still very limited and the most we could manage was a week in Blackpool, but we were determined to make the trip as enjoyable as possible and so took the car to enable us to visit the Lake District as well. Gwynne's Mum joined us and we hired an apartment just off North Promenade, near to Bispham, which was close enough to the town centre yet sufficiently far away to avoid the noise. The children loved the illuminations and an evening trip along the Promenade became the norm for a few nights.

As usual with holidays it seemed no time at all before we found ourselves back on the ferry and approaching Douglas Harbour in the early evening. We were all on deck to watch the berthing of the steamer.

We saw what appeared to be a gorse fire in the area near to Port Jack, but initially took little notice of it. We soon take note, however, of the police and ambulance sirens which seemed to be all over the place when we were driving up to our home.

We had just arrived home when the phone rang - it was the *Examiner* Office. There had been a serious fire at Summerland. That was the "gorse fire" we had spotted from the deck of the steamer. I went to the office where all hell had broken loose. The fire was much worse than at first thought - there were many casualties, most of them tourists.

Summerland was a new attraction built on the site of the old Derby Castle hotel - where I had had my stag night. The intention was to provide covered accommodation for visitors and to provide them with as many attractions inside the structure as possible. In an effort to make the structure as light as possible and to give an effect of actually being outdoors, the architects had decided to use Oroglas, a new plastic type of material for the main walls and part of the roof. Inside the temperature was maintained at a warm level, again to impart the feeling of summer air.

The five floors had many attractions. There was a miniature golf course, many areas for resting, eating and drinking, a children's playground, a large dance area and, all in all, facilities for around 10,000 people at a time.

The whole thing had been burnt to the ground. There were around 130 casualties of which 50 poor souls lost their lives. The emergency services of the Island were stretched to the limit, and there were many instances of bravery from onlookers and passers-by.

The newspaper needed to contribute in some way and we decided that we would publish emergency editions with regular updates on the death toll and the injury list. We worked throughout the night bringing our last edition out at nine o'clock the following morning. The newspaper staff were incredible that night - perhaps we were all hit by the enormity of the event and by the way in which the Manx people contributed towards the rescue operations.

The church hall of St George's was opposite the *Examiner* building in Hill Street. It was decided that it would serve as a morgue and we could easily see from the office windows the number of bodies, many of them small and obviously children, which were brought there. It was awful and was a night which stuck in the minds of Manx people for many, many years. The grief of the families and, indeed, of the Manx nation was not helped by the national press who swarmed over the town and the site seeking every angle to the story and ensuring that it ran for many weeks after the disaster.

PART of my brief at the *Examiner* was to attempt to expand the general printing throughput. By far the largest proportion of printing work and equipment had been left in Athol Street and was now run by Michael Devitt, but there were a couple of presses in Hill Street which could be productive and we began to ask around for business.

I knew that prior to the move to Hill Street, the Palace Hotel & Casino had been customers of the company and that they had not continued that association with Devitt. I had also got wind of a new arrival at the Palace who, I understood, had been brought in to run Palace Travel, their retail agency, and a new inclusive travel company they wanted to launch.

Uninvited, I turned up at the desk of Palace Travel and asked to see this new chap whose name I didn't even know. Brian O'Connor showed me into his new office which, I noted, was still way short of being comfortable. It quickly became apparent that we got on well and a very close business and leisure relationship was formed which remains to this day.

Brian had arrived from Northern Ireland only a few days previously and was in the very early stages of acclimatising himself. He and Rita, his wife, had bought a home in Birch Hill, Onchan where they found peace compared with their previous lives in the war-torn Belfast. They had a daughter, Rita, who was the same age as our youngest, Sarah, and they, too, hit it off immediately.

As part of the Palace Group, Brian launched Golden Isle Holidays, essentially to bring visitors to the Isle of Man. He provided business straight away starting with new stationery, brochures, casino scorecards and menus. The business enabled us to approach other companies and use the Palace work as samples of our quality. The actual main brochure of the new company was too large for us to handle, but we were able to offer advice where needed on aspects of its production.

He wanted to bring in a scheme for the clients of Golden Isle Holidays, whereby they would benefit from discounts offered by local retail outlets. The discounts were gathered together in the form of a book of vouchers and he explained the whole idea to the *Examiner* to see if we could tackle the printing of the discount vouchers. We took the job on and produced "MannCard" - the discount book - for two or three years. It was understood to have been a successful part of Golden Isle's package deal.

Golden Isle went from strength to strength bringing more and more tourists to the Island every year and was a substantial contributor to the Palace revenues until, conscious of its success, the Isle of Man Government suddenly announced it was forming its own inclusive holiday operation - EveryMann Holidays. This was to be directly in opposition to the privately-owned operation and eventually became the cause of Golden Isle's closure. How was that for a classic example of Government participation in the private sector?

There was steady growth in the general printing department. It never became a big operation but it needed some management and Kevin Clarke was recruited to run the department. My brother Nick also joined, moving from Devitt's Athol Street operation to support Kevin.

GWYNNETH and I were broke! The time I had spent off work and the loss of pay hit us very hard. We had no savings and were continually worried about how we would meet our monthly commitments.

Gwynneth decided that she would go to work to help out, but the work had to be such that she was available for the children as much as possible. This meant that whatever work she could do would have to be done either at night or at the weekend. With her maternal instincts an excellent background, she applied for a post in the Jane Crookall Maternity Home as an auxiliary nurse. The hours were Friday and Saturday nights from 8pm-8am for three weeks every month with an additional Sunday once every month. For this, and for being on stand-by in case of sickness in the other staff, she was paid £13 per week!

The extra money was a godsend and we were able, in time, to pay off our debts and to repay the bank who had been most helpful when needed.

Gwynneth continued with the work for two years and enjoyed every minute, but the night shift was not the best arrangement for the mother of a family of four and so when an opportunity arose at Standard Chartered Bank, which fitted in with her scheduling and which she felt she could handle, she applied for and got the job.

WE began to outgrow our home in Westminster Drive. Steven was reaching an age where he needed a bedroom of his own, and whilst Sarah was content to share, the elder two girls were after their own rooms as well. We rather fancied a three-floored property on York Road. It was an elderly house, spacious and substantially built with thick stone walls and a small garden at the side which I visualised for vegetables. As usual for us, it needed some renovation but that was fine.

So we moved. The problem of heating the place suddenly arose. The construction of the property and the fact that it faced north and did not get much sun made the property very cold and something had to be done. We installed a new fire in the lounge with a back boiler to heat radiators - it improved the situation a little but, unfortunately, we had to get used to a cooler environment which stayed with us until our next move.

The photograph below, included with the kind permission of Peter Griffiths, was taken at a retirement presentation to Jim Pooley at the Examiner Office. Jim was a linotype operator and served a considerable time as Branch Secretary of the Typographical Association (the Union). Ron Southall made the presentation and other familiar faces are: Back - Paul Parker, Peter McElroy, Charlie Etchells, Brian Kneen, Roger Oram, Donald Collings, Jim Moore, John Moneta, Ian "Flash" Wrigley, Eric Kinrade, Les Hewitt, Jack Christian, Jack Sillick. Middle - Brian "Tits" Taggart, John Watterson, Peter "Pineapple" Griffiths, Mark Adams, Mark Dudley, John Bostock, Roly Houghton, Dave Welsh, Alan Parrock. Front - Kenny Strickett, Jim Pooley, Ron Southall, Paul Chatel.

CHAPTER TWENTY-SIX

Promotion?

HERBERT Quayle had always suffered from angina and I often used to catch him sucking one of his "bombs" - a pill he took to ease the pain when needed. Stress was the cause of most of his attacks and he began to realise that unless he reduced his workload they would continue and probably get worse.

At a meeting with him and H L Dor, he announced to me that he was standing down as Managing Director and that he was becoming Life-President of the company.

He said that he had discussed the matter with HL and that they wanted me to take over his Managing Director's duties. There would be a small increase in my salary but, of course, I needed to realise that times were hard and it was all that could be afforded at the time.

Rather stupidly, probably conscious of the title, I accepted.

There was no letter of appointment. Despite my requests for it, the "promotion" was never properly announced, and the move did little to improve my position in the company despite the fact that, in theory at least, I was now in charge of the whole thing. I often wondered if the matter had ever been discussed at Board level and whether my appointment as Director was ever recorded. In retrospect, I questioned whether the lack of an announcement was intentional so that if things didn't work out, HL could appoint someone else as Managing Director without any claim from me.

Anyway, I got to attend Board meetings. They were a pantomime in themselves. They were held in Dor's apartment in Mount Bradda with the attendees, normally Herbert, HL, the company secretary Sam Craine and myself. Sometimes Eric Kinrade, the editor, would attend, and other times the gathering would be boosted by a representative of the accountants or the firm's advocates.

My first experience was one to remember. Everyone was given a drink on arrival and after a short time we sat around a rather beautiful dining table. I put my glass down so that I could pull out my chair - wrong!!

"Would you mind please using a table mat for your glass?" says HL. And he left his own seat, took out a handkerchief and wiped the table where I had put my glass!

Sam Craine managed a very ironic smile and passed me a table mat.

Frankly, the Board meetings were a farce. I began to realise that they were merely an exercise to satisfy the company minutes. The fact was that HL owned the company and whatever he wanted he got. Thus, when the circulation of the newspaper had risen to its highest level ever, enabling the advertising boys an easier pitch for sales, HL doubled the cover price of the paper and the circulation halved. When advertising revenue was good and advertisements were filling the newspapers, instead of increasing the pagination, he doubled the advertising rates.

At the Board meetings the only people prepared to speak against such moves were Sam and myself, but it was invariably a lost cause and we lost heart after a while.

I was struck by a bad attack of hepatitis and jaundice at the same time and it meant my isolation in Noble's Hospital for a fortnight and a three-week convalescence. It was normal for hourly paid staff who could claim overtime pay for additional hours not to receive pay whilst ill. I was amazed when despite my salaried employment I, too, didn't get paid for the time I was off.

HL came to visit me in hospital. He brought me a gift presuming it would make me feel better . . . it was a copy of *Roget's Thesaurus!!* Bloody hell - did I need that!

Dor's desire to become the only newspaper proprietor on the Isle of Man was always uppermost in his mind and when Ramsey advocate John Christian became the proprietor of the *Ramsey Courier*, changed its name to *Isle of Man Courier* and moved the firm's premises to Ridgeway Street, Douglas, Dor immediately tried to buy it from him. Had his price been reasonable, John may well have been happy to sell as he did not specifically wish to own a newspaper but, typical of HL, he wanted it for next to nothing and John Christian rebuffed him on many occasions.

On Friday one particular week, HL asked me what I was doing the following afternoon as he wondered if I would be good enough to accompany him on a "local trip". I said that it all depended upon what the "trip" entailed.

"Well I need to go to Ramsey," he said.

I immediately knew that this was another approach to John Christian.

"OK, but we'll be wasting our time unless the price is right!"

The following afternoon he collected me from home and we drove to a point near to where I knew John Christian lived. Assuming that the meeting was to be at John's home, I enquired as to what time it had been arranged?

"Oh, I haven't arranged anything," said HL. "I want you to call on him unexpectedly!"

"What? You expect him to fall for an unexpected approach from me? Do you really think he will listen to anything I say."

"He may," said HL. "It's worth a try - he may respond to a message that you think he should sell. I'll sit here whilst you're indoors."

I should really have told him where to go but I was so taken aback at his cheek, I actually called on John.

"Hello, Colin," a very friendly greeting from John Christian, as always from my point of view, "what brings you here?"

"I just want a word, John."

"Come in, come in, and have a drink."

I swear he knew immediately why I was there, but he let me explain that it was my view that he should listen to HL's approaches, that he should negotiate the best deal possible and that he divest himself from newspapers as it was obvious that they should not be part of his business portfolio.

"Why didn't he come himself?" said John with a grin. "I wouldn't be surprised if he's sat in the car around the corner!"

We both burst out laughing.

"Look," said John, "I have no desire to own a newspaper, as you well know, but I'm damned if I'm going to allow that man to develop a complete monopoly in the industry in the Isle of Man. I'm afraid it's pure devilment on my part, but I'm not selling and, please, tell him that."

I did exactly that and related word for word what John had told me. We drove back to Douglas in silence - what a waste of an afternoon!

SOME old friends of my family lived in Inverness and had always been keen for us to visit them. So, in 1978 we put a roof rack on our old Datsun estate car, piled it high and all six of us, plus Gwynneth's Mum, crammed in for the journey by steamer to Ardrossan and then a long drive up to the capital of the Highlands.

Gwynneth Jr showing her expertise in photography during our trip to Inverness! Tracey, at rear, Steven and Sarah along with our two family friends, Betty and Alistair McKenzie.

It was an eventful trip. We drove over in the Edinburgh direction and crossed the Forth Bridge where there was a sign reading 'Beware - Cross Winds'.

Associating 'cross' with a state of mind, seven-year-old Sarah announ-ces, "I don't like the look of those cross winds, Mum."

We enjoyed a lovely break in Scotland, did a lot of touring around and visited all the well-known visitor attractions.

AT WORK, this period made me think long and hard about the future - would I ever be able to properly manage the company with HL interfering all the time? Was I being adequately paid for the time I spent there? The answers to these points all seemed to be negative and I began to despair.

Despite the fact that he still attended St Mary's every day for mid-day Mass and professed to have caring thoughts as a true Catholic, HL seemed to have no comprehension of the worries and the concerns of the staff and their families. One classic example of this came about when we were dis-cussing the annual wage claim which had been lodged by the union for the forthcoming year. It wasn't actually a large claim - it covered the cost of liv-ing increase and a bit more but it was far from excessive.

"It's not a big claim, " I said, "and if the membership accepts, we should meet the claim straight away."

"Oh, no," said HL. "it's much more than necessary and we can't afford it."

"That's not so, Mr Dor. It barely covers the cost of living increase and we have already increased the cover price of the paper to help towards it."

"The cost of living increase!" he said. "What cost of living increase? There has been no increase in the cost of living - for example, I paid my laun-dry bill last week and noted it was the same as the previous year!"

I pointed out to him that he was very fortunate that he was able to make use of the services of a laundry and that most of his employees' wives could not afford a machine to do their own washing.

He was quite taken aback and I walked out. The man lived in a dream world!!

I became good pals with Sam Craine. He was another enigma - you never know how you would find him and invariably any conversation would commence with Sam in his blackest mood. There were particular people in the company he disliked, feeling they were not contributing, yet drawing large salaries. He had a downer on all journalists, though we always laughed as, when tackled about who would write if they weren't there, he had no answer. Probably it was our joint efforts at the Board meetings which drew us togeth-er. We spent many moments discussing the latest madcap idea of HL and we had fixed ideas on what we would do if the company belonged to us - the first move would be to fire HL!!

It was Sam who pointed out to me the fact that my salary was ridiculous when the responsibilities of the position were taken into account. He pointed out that I was actually receiving less as MD than a typesetter was receiving after he had been paid his overtime.

I made a mental note and tackled HL about it a few days later. He accepted the points I made - he had no option as I had brought in pay slips showing the comparison - but he amazed me by claiming that I should be satisfied with the fact that I was in a position of power.

"I see you," he said, "as the future Cecil King of the Isle of Man!"

The future Cecil King . . . I couldn't believe it!

Cecil King had been the Chairman of the Mirror Group of newspapers in the UK and, in fairness, had been for many years in a position where he could almost dictate which party should form the next UK government, such had been the power of the *Daily Mirror*. Comparing me with Cecil King was utterly ludicrous and I told him so.

"No," he said, "it's right. Look at those people in Manx history who had press power and affected decisions of the Manx Government."

"Yes," I retorted, "and don't forget they invariably owned the press and look what happened to some of them, indeed, some ended up in jail!"

The man was far from an idiot but, hell, sometimes he ran it close!

HL'S DESIRE to own the *Ramsey Courier* and John Christian's refusal to sell created a situation whereby all connections between *Ramsey Courier* and the *Examiner* were frowned upon.

The *Courier* had appointed Paul Gaskell as their Advertising Manager. He had come to the Island from Lancashire and had experience in newspaper advertising and in promotion. Paul set about raising the *Courier's* revenue and profile. We came into contact regularly - he was aggressive but he was also very loyal and Paul became a good friend.

Their printing plant was very unreliable and, when it let them down one publishing day, I took a call from Paul to see if we would print the issue for them.

We did, and HL was not happy. "Why did you print it," he said.

"Because they paid good money for the service and it didn't damage us to do it."

Paul Gaskell was recruited by John Christian from Lancashire to take over the advertising management and general promotion of the Ramsey Courier. Paul became a very good friend.

"But you don't know that," he said. "If they begin to lose issues, people will lose faith in them and they could close down."

Shortly after that episode we were hit with the bombshell that the *Courier* had been bought by *Halifax Courier*. Obviously they had offered John Christian a realistic price and, true to his word, he had sold. The *Courier* continued for a short while printing on the Island but the superior quality of the company's presses in Yorkshire prevailed and the printing switched to the UK.

Paul Gaskell, however, remained regularly in contact with me, on occasions when bad weather interfered with the delivery of their paper from Yorkshire, requesting assistance, with us providing it whenever we could. Not too long afterwards, the *Isle of Man Courier,* as it had been renamed, became a free issue.

SOON my discontent was becoming obvious and, with the four of us on a night out, Brian O'Connor tackled me about it. I told him all the problems I was having including my poor salary.

"Frankly you need to be in business where you can benefit from its success," he said. "You're never going to be in that position at the *Examiner*, despite all HL's insinuations."

I knew that he was right but I also knew that to start a business, especially in printing, was an expensive exercise and required money I did not have.

"I know," said Brian, "but there are other ways you could achieve it."

He went on to tell me about a guy he knew quite well, who was also from Northern Ireland and who had interests in security companies and air taxis, as well as a major share in a graphic design company.

" I don't know if he would be interested," said Brian, "but the design company would be a perfect fit for a printing company wouldn't it? It's worth a try - do you want me to set up a meeting?"

The meeting was set up for two weeks hence and I needed to spend some time with the two people with whom I had been discussing my discontent over the past few months. I related to Kevin Clarke and my brother everything I had discussed with Brian. They were up for any move which would see them out of the *Examiner* and in business for themselves.

The three of us met with Stewart Jamieson in the Shore Hotel at Gansey in early 1979. and it was another life-changing moment . . .

CHAPTER TWENTY-SEVEN

A Chance to Strike Out?

S TEWART Jamieson, was a self-made, wealthy entrepreneur with very good connections in Northern Ireland. He was involved heavily in the security business and was the principal of Security Centres - one of the largest operators in the province. In addition he owned and operated City Air Links which was a small air charter operation based at Ronaldsway. When he detailed his background and his connections, he mentioned that it

was his intention to eventually take Security Centres to the London Stock Exchange and have it floated as a public company - a move which would make him a vast amount of money.

We related our unrest to Stewart and explained to him that we had investigated the possibility of setting up a printing operation in the Island. We knew that, providing certain criteria were met, Isle of Man Government grants were available for capital investment, for marketing and for start-up. It was not the Government's intention to encourage the further division of local work, the new project would have to show that it would be bringing in new business.

Stewart explained that he owned a graphic design company in Belfast. It was headed up by Des Bingham who was assisted by a couple of account managers. The company had very good connections, particular-

Stewart Jamieson was a successful businessman with growing companies in Ulster and a desire to float them on the London Stock Exchange at the earliest opportunity.

ly with Stewarts - a supermarket group - and a number of other prominent businesses around the Belfast area. He was very confident that all of the work presently handled by the company could move to the Isle of Man and that he would arrange for it to happen.

The fact that any new project of this nature could be supported by grants from the Isle of Man Government was an important aspect for Stewart, but we were keen to emphasise the need for new business to be brought in to the Manx printing industry for such grants to become available.

We discussed at length the different types of business presently handled in Belfast and it appeared that certainly most of the work would be familiar to us and should not present a problem for the new operation.

It was debatable whether or not the Government grants would actually apply to second-hand equipment and for this reason we were of the view that it would be necessary to buy new printing machinery. We explained that whilst we would dearly love to purchase Heidelberg or Roland kit - top of the range at the time - we realised the funding necessary would be too high and so we had identified Swedish Solna presses as our target.

We reached the point where the new business ownership had to be discussed. Stewart explained that, as he would be the financier, he would not be interested in any deal which gave him less than a 75% ownership. He also pointed out that, as he would expect me to be the Managing Director, my portion should be 15% and the remaining 10% should be divided equally between Nick and Kevin.

At the close of the meeting, Stewart asked us had we thought of any names for the new printing company?

"We have tossed a few names around," I said, "and the best we have come up with is The Print Centre."

None of the three of us were particularly impressed with the name, but Stewart thought it great.

"OK, but let's make it Print Centres." he said, "After all, we don't intend to restrict the operation to one!"

We were happy to agree to such a positive request and we agreed that, to allow the three of us to reflect on what had been discussed, we would meet with Stewart again in a week's time

The three of us left the meeting in a buoyant mood, feeling that we had an opportunity at last to take a big step towards owning our own printing operation, and we began to make plans.

I RELATED to Gwynneth everything that had been discussed with Stewart. As usual, she was very supportive mainly because she was aware how unsettled I had become at the *Examiner*. We discussed how we could raise the cash needed for my 15% - the only method open to us was to raise the mortgage on our home - and we agreed that we should go down this path when it was required.

We met again with Stewart a week later and advised him that we wished to proceed and that we were happy with all of the matters discussed and agreed at the previous meeting.

"Excellent!" said Stewart, "I will set the ball in motion at my end and you guys can continue the work needed for the application to Government for the grants. By the way, do you know my accountant, Charles Fargher?"

Whilst I had actually met with Charles' father, Jack, who was a highly respected accountant and the senior in J G Fargher & Co., I didn't know Charles, and so it was arranged that we would meet in the near future. It was quite a significant meeting as well, as Charles became one of my closest friends and was a business partner of my brother and myself for many years.

The next couple of months were difficult for all three of us. For my part, I had to try to concentrate on my work at the *Examiner* whilst, whenever possible, have meetings and make arrangements which related to our new venture. It can't have been easy for Nick and Kevin either - it was vital that we all remained tight-lipped about the future.

I met with Ken Bawden, then the Secretary of the Government's Board of Industry. Ken's elder brother, Arthur, was also a civil servant at that time - Clerk to the Legislative Council, actually - and he had been a classmate of mine at St Ninian's many years previously. Ken explained how keen the Board was to assist in new manufacturing ventures and I was happy to detail the conversations we had with Stewart. Whilst Ken was most careful not to give any assurances, I got the distinct impression that we would be successful with our grant application.

The three of us looked at a number of different sites for the plant to be located. It was important that access was good as large truck deliveries would be made, and most of those we viewed were not too good in this respect. We then decided to speak to Isle of Man Industrial Development Ltd - a Manx offshoot of John Finlan, a large construction company in Cheshire. They were developing an industrial complex at Spring Valley. The company was headed up by Leslie Vondy who was chairman and he was supported by Charlie Farrell who was based in Cheshire and mainly worked for the Finlan operation there.

We were shown Unit Nine which was vacant. The height of the building was far in excess of what we had sought, the rent was more than we had anticipated but the floor area was about right. We discussed the matter briefly with Brian O'Connor and we decided to go ahead.

The time came to produce the cash we needed. Gwynneth asked a few questions at Standard Chartered and, as she was a good employee, they

Our stepfather, John, has been a Freemason for many years and has served in most capacities within his Lodge. The family supported him at the Grand Master's Dinner.

offered to fund our needs at a very attractive interest rate available only to staff. Nick and Kevin had fixed up their investments and so it was now all go.

During my time at the *Examiner* I had developed an excellent trading relationship with Malcolm Powell who headed up the paper supply firm of Powell and Heilbron based in Liverpool. After a period of uncertainty with Bowaters, who had supplied newsprint reels to the newspaper for years, Malcolm stepped in with a much more attractive price and a greater degree of security.

Malcolm assured the three of us that Powell and Heilbron would supply the new venture with all varieties of paper and was kind enough to allow us very good trading terms to assist us in the early stages. His offer was genuine and most supportive and it formed the basis of a friendship which continues to this day in our retirement.

We decided the company would begin operations on 1 November 1979.

CHAPTER TWENTY-EIGHT

Striking Out

I TOLD Herbert Quayle I was leaving. He was disappointed, but when I explained what we were going to do, he congratulated me and wished us all the best. He mentioned that we may well find it difficult as business was in something of a depression, of which I was aware, but also said that if we could work our way through that we should be well set for the future. True to type, Herbert said that he was looking forward to us "giving B&Hx a run for their money!"

Dor was a different matter.

"You're mad," he said. "You won't last six months."

And that was it. Typical.

All that did was to make the three of us even more determined to succeed.

THE installations went well and by the 1 November we were ready to start production.

I had heard of some equipment which was lying dormant in the Ridgeway Street offices of the *Isle of Man Courier*. I managed to get a viewing and thought that we could certainly make use of the Heidleberg cylinder press that was there along with some other ancillary equipment. I made an offer which I felt would definitely be rejected and was amazed to be advised it had been accepted and when could it be moved? We moved it quickly enough!

The first job off the press was a menu for Tony Woodrow, then manager at the Palace Hotel and a good friend of ours. The first colour job was a print of Mike Hailwood, the TT star, which had been painted by Peter Hearsey who was making a name for himself in Manx art circles.

My old friend at the *Courier,* Paul Gaskell, had joined the Palace Group in charge of promotions and was keen to use the new company as much as possible.

We became busy rather quickly and before too long we had to take on an apprentice to help with the pre-press work, and a bindery operative to

The responsibilities within Print Centres were such that, while Nick looked after the machine room and bindery production, Kevin (above left) was in charge of the origination department. He was supported by Alan Perkin (above right) who joined as an apprentice and, later, by Mike Betteridge who operated a computer typesetter.

handle the finishing work we had to undertake. Alan Perkin was the apprentice and it's worth noting that he remains to this day, an important part of the company's success. Judy Bennett took on the bindery work and she remained with the company for many years until her retirement. Ann Lancaster, who all three of us got to know when she was working in the reception office of the *Examiner*, joined us to look after all our office work and accounts.

ONE interesting anecdote were the differing reactions of Herbert Quayle and H L Dor to Print Centres going into production. Herbert came up to see us two or three times and was always keen to know how we were getting on - perhaps reporting back, but we thought: so what? One night around eight o'clock, Nick was operating the press and suddenly realised he was not alone in the building. He looked round and realised Dor was in the middle of the unit just gazing around.

"Hello, Mr Dor," said Nick, "you gave me a bit of a shock."

"Amazing," answered Dor and promptly walked out!

THE first six months were hectic, but the work was there. My main concern, however, centred around the fact that the volume of work from Belfast had not materialised, despite a number of visits of mine to their premises in Belfast and visits by Des and his account managers to the Isle of Man. This lack of UK work could easily prevent us receiving the Government grant and I continually referred this to Stewart.

"It'll come," he kept saying - and he always had a reason why it hadn't happened to date.

I felt that Stewart was genuinely sincere in his original claim to be able to supply work to us from the Belfast agency - but the three of us began to realise that the real reason was that he did not have as much influence over Des Bingham and his managers as he thought. They had their own favourite print companies in Belfast who they trusted and were happy with and they did not see why they should be directed to supply a company miles away whose work, in their eyes, may not be as good. When all is said and done, the fact that Stewart Jamieson had a stake in a company in the Isle of Man was of no concern to them and they certainly weren't set to benefit as a result.

We did get some work - I recall an enormous order for Stewart's supermarket which involved the printing of coupons and then the gathering of them together to form a booklet. The job was so time-consuming that all of our wives were involved at some point as well as us and, as we had to meet a price dictated to us by the agency, we questioned the viability of it.

We were determined to make sure that we knew all the time how well or how badly the company was operating. Charles Fargher produced monthly figures and we held a Board meeting every month. Some months the numbers were good, some months they were awful and when they were not good and Stewart wasn't happy, the three of us always referred to the fact that, up to now, he had not produced the work he had promised and the throughput of business was the result of our efforts locally.

After a long delay, we eventually received notice that our grant application had been approved, but we were of the view that this had only happened because of our own efforts, not because the UK work had materialised, because it hadn't.

We were some eighteen months into the new company's operations when, at a Board meeting, Stewart again laid into us over the monthly figures. The turnover had not reached the budgeted figure and there was a deficit on the bottom line. He went mad and we, in turn, retaliated. The meeting broke up in total disharmony.

The three of us were getting sick of this . . . we were doing our bit, Stewart had not produced the goods and yet we were bearing the brunt. It couldn't go on.

We asked ourselves what was the point in continuing with the present situation - it was not what we had hoped for, as far as our own company was concerned, and we were sick of the arguments.

We decided to act. I took the bull by the horns one afternoon early in 1981 and drove to meet with Stewart in his office at the airport.

He was very amenable when I arrived and we both sat down with a cup of coffee. He asked how things were going and I told him of our dissatisfaction and that it couldn't go on.

"We want a break-up of the partnership," I told him.

He went berserk, thumping his desk and shouting at the top of his voice. I stood up expecting to be clouted at any minute, but I stood my ground and later, when the afternoon's proceedings finally sunk in, I was quite proud of myself.

Eventually he calmed and started talking normally but, strangely, not about Print Centres. In fact, Print Centres was not mentioned again that afternoon.

"Do you fancy a whisky," said Stewart. We sat down with our drinks.

"I've bought a new house, you know," he said.

"I know, up at Ballakilpheric - you must be above the snow line there," I joked.

More whisky.

"Yep, 'course I've had to do a lot to it," he said, "and it's a bloody mess at the moment."

I asked if it could be seen from his office window and he pointed it our to me. "It looks good to me," I said, happy that the conversation was about his property.

More whisky.

"Tell you what," he said. "let's go and see it and you can have a proper look at it then."

Astonished I got up, rather gingerly, and we walked to our cars.

How I managed to drive to Ballakilpheric and then back home I will never know, but one thing is for sure, I would certainly have failed any tests for drunkenness and I am ashamed each time I relate the story.

The following morning we received legal notification from Stewart's advocates that he would resist any break-up of the partnership and that he would sue us if we persisted.

Great!

The next six months were horrific - we resisted all Stewart's demands for a Board meeting as we were aware that he intended to appoint a couple of people to the Board who he knew he could depend upon to support him which would negate our superior strength in numbers at that level. Aware of the numbers needed for quorums, etc., we went to great lengths to be "absent from the Island" on occasions when he tried to have an Annual General

Meeting. It was ridiculous - we were as determined as he was to succeed but it wasn't doing me much good from a health point of view. And we still had a firm to run!

After a conversation with Charles Fargher, I was delighted when he offered to use his association with Stewart to try to resolve the problem. Charles came back to us with an offer from Stewart which was the amount he wanted to walk away. It took our breath away and I suspect that even Charles was of the view that it was "rather large". I advised Charles that we would not be able to raise that amount of cash and he agreed to go back to Stewart and try to reduce the figure to a more realistic level.

Charles was successful and we settled on a figure which, to the three of us, seemed enormous but, regrettably that was the price we had to pay and we began to make arrangements to raise the cash between us.

In those days, business was a lot more pleasurable and trusting than it is today. Contact with your bank manager, for example, was made via a friendly 'phone call, whereas now bank staff are moved so often, you are fortunate indeed if you know, actually, who is your bank manager!

This was so important to me that I didn't hesitate and went straight

John Sayle.

to the top. John Sayle was the Isle of Man Bank's General Manager - I knew him and his Assistant Manager John Allen, for that matter, from my membership at Peel Golf Club where John Sayle was a prominent official. They were both approachable and genuinely nice guys.

I briefed John on what was about to occur. He, of course, knew Stewart well.

"This is really good news," said John. "I'm very pleased for you."

"Thanks, John, but it's a hell of a lot of money," I replied.

"It is," said John, "but you will be free to operate the company as you wish and we will help as much as we can with that both personally and corporately - I'm assuming that you will be the majority shareholder?"

That was a point which I had not even considered.

"Well, we would certainly be looking for that," said John.

John Allen.

John Allen was working in his office next door. John Sayle rang through and asked him to come in for a chat. The three of us then proceed-

Charles Fargher - he was surprised to be asked to remain as a director, but became a very good friend and colleague.

ed to go over all that had happened over the past few months. It was wonderful to have the knowledge that we would be supported in the takeover and I began, at last, to feel it was all worthwhile.

WHILST the buy-out from Stewart was a big step forward for us and absolutely the right thing to do, the enormity of what we were taking on began to hit home.

From our point of view, Gwynneth and I risked everything - any small amount of savings and our home were used as collateral. I'm sure that the same applied to both Nick and Kevin. It didn't do to dwell on the situation and the obvious need was for us all to look forward and make a success of the venture.

The first action we took was to ask Charles Fargher if he would stay with us as Finance Director. I laughed at Charles' obvious surprise when he was asked as it was so obviously unexpected. As he later admitted, as far as he was concerned he assumed that we viewed him as part of the "opposition" for the past few months. However, we took the view that if it hadn't been for him, the deadlock with Stewart would have continued, and that alone warranted some recognition. Anyway, we still required to be kept in line from a financial point of view, and he was efficient in this area.

I visited Ken Bawden and briefed him. Ken was understanding and assured me that the Industry Board would still continue to support us, but he did request that we maintained a search for UK business and I readily agreed.

We then began a period of consolidation during which we set out to properly establish the company as a dependable, competitive print operation run by people who were friendly and efficient.

We met with Malcolm Powell who was our major paper supplier and he once again assured us of his support.

We needed to expand our pre-press as Kevin and Alan Perkin were coming under pressure. Simon Brown joined us to look after that side of things. Gary Allen became our first employee in the machine room assisting Nick in production. We were beginning to make headway.

We were approached by a retired resident of the Island to see if we were interested in the production of a magazine with which he retained a connection. The magazine turned out to be *Taxi Times* which was produced monthly for circulation to all London black cab drivers. We printed a number of issues but the publishers eventually preferred to have it produced closer to London and the contract moved away.

I DIDN'T feel too great. I had a pain which would not go away and, in fact, got worse over a few hours. I went home. It was so damned painful that I didn't even bother to take my coat off - I just needed to sit down and rest.

On our first continental holiday to Majorca - with Brian and Rita O'Connor.

When Gwynneth arrived home from her work, I apparently did not look too great and she suggested I go to bed. I had a job getting up the stairs, by this time the pain, mainly located below my right armpit, was awful. Gwynneth wasn't taking any chances - she called the doctor.

When he arrived he asked all the normal questions and then asked if I had had any other problems of late. I told him about the varicose veins I had suffered from for years, and the phlebitis which had been diagnosed when I went to my GP the week previous with inflammation in my lower leg. He then announced that he thought I may have had a deep vein thrombosis and that he thought I should be in hospital. He went to call the ambulance and I stopped him saying Gwynneth would take me - that was a much more attractive thought. He agreed and then left. Two minutes after he had gone, he was back.

"No," he said, "I can't allow you to go in a car - it would be too dangerous. You must go in the ambulance."

Charming!

The ambulance duly came and I was admitted and diagnosed with a pulmonary embolism - a blood clot in my lung. I was immediately put on a drip and the pain started to recede. Altogether I was two weeks in Noble's and a further three weeks off work. I was told how fortunate I had been - if the clot had stuck in the heart my problem would have been terminal!

The events of the previous months, I was told, almost certainly contributed to the problem. The advice was to take things much easier.

OUR friendship with Brian and Rita had continued and Brian's efforts at the Palace Group were bringing results. In addition to Golden Isle Holidays bringing people into the Island he had introduced the innovative idea of providing a service which enabled Island residents to fly directly to Majorca and the Costa del Sol from Ronaldsway.

This was a great idea and was strongly supported by those involved in the tourism business as the dates had been purposefully arranged for the end of the Isle of Man's season.

The four of us decided to take advantage as well - Sarah and Rita joined us on the first trip we made - to Majorca. It was very successful and all of us had the time of our lives. It was, actually, the very first time Gwynneth and myself had been abroad and required a passport - quite a milestone. The holiday was particularly memorable for the return trip which, according to the departures board at Palma airport, was scheduled to land at JURBY! The trip itself, particularly for us novices at "long distance" air travel, was rather odd as, when we approached our destination at either end, rather than a steady descent to the airport, the aircraft seemed to drop like a stone - disconcerting to say the least.

The following year we decided we would go again - this time to the Costa del Sol. I remember asking Brian to check the name of the airline as, "there was no way I want to fly with the same lot as last year."

"It's OK," he came back, "I've checked - it's a different airline."

We got on the aircraft, settled into our seats and took off. Shortly afterwards I happened to turn over the small cover on the head rest of the seat in front and there, on the reverse, was the name of the previous year's airline. So much for change!

In 1980, we decided to take Gwynneth's Mum on a coach tour to Kranska Gora, then part of Yugoslavia and on the border with Italy - it was the first time, at the age of 80, that Annie had obtained a passport. We all enjoyed every minute of the trip - even the food we had in France, where at dinner one evening in a rather loud voice, Annie proudly proclaimed the meat to be, "Horsemeat! They do eat horsemeat in France you know!"

AUNTIE Ethel had always been a very strong supporter of me and always claimed that whatever I set out to do, I would achieve. Of course, this wasn't always so, but I appreciated her confidence in me.

She had been failing for some time, however. She had developed a bad case of osteoporosis and was often in considerable pain. Suddenly she became particularly ill and the doctor whisked her straight into hospital. Her heart had failed and they had difficulty in discerning a regular beat.

She died peacefully two days after her 73rd birthday.

CHAPTER TWENTY-NINE

Venture into Publishing

IN 1982, Manx Airlines, an Isle of Man operation funded by British Midland, began services to the Island and quickly gained support from the Manx population. The first flights were in late 1982 using a Bandeirante aircraft and in the following year that equipment was supported by a Vickers Viscount which became a favourite of regular passengers to the Island for many years.

The airline was headed up by Terry Liddiard as Managing Director supported by Tim Stevens as Marketing Manager and the team set about expanding the company as quickly as possible. One of Terry's first actions was to introduce an in-flight magazine for his passengers and he recruited Eunice Salmond, who was still writing under the name of "Fenella" for the newspaper, as editor of the magazine.

A competition was held to decide a name for the magazine and many suggestions were submitted - the winning submission was from a Manx lady who suggested that the magazine be called *Manx Tails*. Her reasoning was linked to the Manx Airlines' aircraft all of which had been painted with a large "Three Legs of Man" symbol on the aircrafts' tail, coupled with the assumption that the magazine would include "tales" of the Isle of Man.

The first issue of *Manx*

Managing Director, Terry Liddiard was always very keen to promote the local aspect of Manx Airlines.

Tails was printed in Nottingham. I thought that this was a really bad move for an operation which claimed to be wholly Manx and I remarked upon this in a telephone call to Eunice.

"I agree with you," said Eunice. "Why don't you go and make the same complaint to Terry Liddiard?"

Perhaps if I had given the matter a bit of thought I might have treaded a bit more carefully in anticipation of a reaction, but no, a meeting was duly arranged with Terry Liddiard.

He was immediately likeable. He was the sort of person who was invariably busy and up to his neck in all sorts of problems, but he could still find time to talk to you.

I introduced myself and gave Terry a run-down on Print Centres and how we would be happy to undertake printing work for the airline. He was receptive and promised to pass the word around to his colleagues who were handling various printed work.

As the meeting drew to a close. I remarked how good I thought the new magazine appeared.

"But I'm really disappointed," I said, "that Manx Airlines went to Nottingham to have it printed rather than the Isle of Man."

"Could you produce it then?" Terry asked.

"Yes, we would love to - and I've worked with Eunice previously." I told him about the *Examiner* office.

"That's fine," said Terry, "you guys can take over for the next issue. But there is one big thing . . ."

I thought - I knew it, there has to be a catch.

"I'm not selling the advertisements," announced Terry, "so you'll have to arrange for somebody to do it for you or do it yourselves! And we will need to have some form of contract"

I suspected later that, for the first issue, Terry had been forced to sell the advertisements and had not liked it one bit.

"I'll organise that

"Manx Tails" was our first publishing venture - the magazine will this year celebrate 30 years of unbroken publication.

with pleasure," I said, and walked out of the office with a big smile. It was the beginning of a very happy and productive relationship for both companies which lasted almost twenty years and was the nucleus of our company's publishing activities from that day forward.

REALITY reared its head! Who the hell was going to sell the advertisements? I had experience working with advertising sales people but I had never sold an "ad" in my life.

It was obvious that with the magazine being produced only four times a year, we certainly could not afford to employ anybody solely for that purpose.

So, as I had been selling print for a while, there was little alternative but for me to take it on.

Actually, I enjoyed it.

It was a new medium for the Isle of Man and quite a few local companies were keen to be seen in the issue. With the promotion of the finance sector gaining momentum and the acceptance that this magazine would be the first publication about the Island seen by air travellers, the number of professional companies and those associated with finance, who wished to advertise with us, grew very quickly.

To cope with the business element of the magazine and to ensure its separation from the general content, we quickly introduced *Money Media* as the business section of *Manx Tails* and printed it on entirely different paper so that the separation would be very apparent. It worked a treat and both parts of the magazine expanded rapidly.

STEVE DeHaven was an American who had married a Manx girl. He was employed at Manx Radio as an advertising representative and so we came into regular contact whilst out on business. Steve was a religious guy and was heavily involved in the Unity School of Christianity which was based in America but had branches all over the world. Steve sat on the Council of the UK branch which was based in Maidenhead, Berkshire.

At the time, Manx Radio were transmitting small sound bites at regular intervals called *The Word for Today* which consisted of an explanation and definition of a different word every day with the word invariably having a religious connection.

Steve approached us to see if we were interested in tendering for the booklet from which each *Word for Today* was taken. *The Word* is a small publication which had a monthly print requirement of around 14,000 copies and contained 36 pages stapled at the spine. At the time, they were being printed in the USA and sent by freight to Maidenhead, but Steve was of the view that savings could be made if we were to print them on the Island. In company

with Steve, I visited Maidenhead and met with David Davenport who was running operations at the Branch office. David was very keen on the move as it would mean that he could personalise *The Word* with the Maidenhead address rather than the US address which was contained on the imported booklets.

We did our sums, they did theirs and Steve was right.

The original film used for the printing of *The Word* in the US was sent to us from their headquarters, invariably being opened by customs who always confused Unity Church with another organisation which was not in favour at the time. We amended the film to suit David Davenport, printed the magazine and shipped to Maidenhead. The finished magazines, carrying our Isle of Man imprint, were then circulated using their mailing list, throughout the world. It was a brilliant arrangement which has, to my knowledge, carried on from 1983 and remains firmly in place.

JOHN Swale, the Lancashire newspaper proprietor whom I had met during my tenure at the *Examiner*, finally lost patience over his treatment by the Merseyside branch of the trade union, and closed the newspaper he had run for many years. John loved the Isle of Man and he and his wife, Vera, had retired to a lovely cottage on the outskirts of Douglas.

Whilst closing the paper, he had retained possession of a number of other publications he had published for many years including an *Annual Directory* for the Liverpool Chamber of Commerce and the maritime magazine *Sea Breezes*.

John came to see us at Spring Valley at our new, enlarged location - we had moved into adjoining units, 28 and 30, and had combined them into one 8,000 sq ft production facility. He wanted to know if we would be interested in printing *Sea Breezes* for him?

Whilst our efforts to bring printing from the UK to satisfy the Department of Industry's request had not been too successful, in *Manx Tails* and *The Word* we had achieved a regular monthly throughput of new business. *Sea Breezes* would boost this even further as it was monthly and consisted of eighty A5 pages with two full colour sections and a print quantity of around 13,000 copies per month.

John was a tough businessman - one of the "old school" so to speak - and a very determined negotiator but, eventually he became happy with our price and we started work on the magazine. In this instance, we had to do all the typesetting, scan the photographs and do all the page make-up prior to printing. Once the job was finished we had to arrange for it to be sent by carrier to Liverpool from where copies were sent out to every wholesale newsagent in the UK and to a number of agents throughout the world. Again our Manx imprint was highly visible.

We also had to envelope and post around 3,500 from our premises to service a subscription list of readers. This had previously been serviced by the UK Postal Services but, now provided good business for Isle of Man Post. At various times later on, in pricing negotiations with Isle of Man Post, we often became frustrated about this and came to

My brother, Nick, discusses various aspects of the 'Sea Breezes" production with John Swale.

the conclusion that the Postal Authority tended to forget that we brought the business to the Island in the first place! Although the magazine is now separately owned, it is still printed by the company and continues to circulate throughout the world.

WHILST all this was good news there were also some instances when our lack of experience got the better of us.

One such time was the telephone call from a resident at the Palace Hotel, a Mr Barry Smith, enquiring if we would be interested in tendering for the printing of a large amount of work for the Government of Micronesia, Hilton Hotels (US) and Continental Airlines.

We thought it was a joke.

But we checked with the Palace, "Yes, a Mr Barry Smith is a resident and has been with us for a couple of days - he's due to check out on Friday."

It was worth a try and Kevin went to meet him as arranged.

He returned with an enormous amount of work, mostly stationery, all of which had to be quoted and submitted before Mr Smith left on Friday.

We had no idea where Micronesia was and questioned whether such a person could be representing Hilton Hotels and Continental Airlines.

We rang him.

He was very pleasant and seemed not to get too upset with our questions which were quite intrusive. He indicated that he had business connections in Micronesia - a collection of islands in Polynesia, South Pacific - and that he travelled there a lot. The connections with Hilton and Continental were merely a result of both companies having a presence on the islands.

We agreed to do the quotes and he agreed to meet us at Print Centres on Thursday afternoon.

It took us half the night to do the quotations.

We met with Mr Smith on the Thursday and went over every one. He queried a few and we compromised, but overall the business was worth around £8,000 and by this time we were keen to take it on. We talked over the method of delivery and listened to his recommendations - he was very experienced and we bowed to his wishes.

We had spoken to the bank who advised that we should obtain a letter of credit before we started work and we raised this with Mr Smith.

"That's only to be expected," he said, "and I will arrange for it straight away. But I would ask that you print me some business cards for me straight away?"

This represented a very small cost compared with the overall order and so we agreed.

"I'm sure that this will be the start of a very successful relationship," he said, and left.

We rubbed our hands.

The letter of credit arrived was met in full and the work was delivered according to his instructions.

A couple of months later we received another call from Mr Smith, now known to us as Barry. He was in Matlock, Derbyshire at what we understood to be his parents' home. He sent us another batch of work, most of which again had to be quoted, and we informed him of the prices and the overall revenue which was roughly the same as the first time.

Again we requested a letter of credit which duly arrived, was met and the work was printed and delivered.

For our third venture, Barry travelled to the Island and met with us. He had a smaller order - around £4,000 - but the work this time was very time-sensitive and he asked if we would be good enough to begin the work whilst he was arranging the letter of credit.

We did - in fact, we had the work completed and there was still no letter of credit.

The work was obviously no good to anyone else, he had come good on two previous occasions, he assured us the money would come, and so we delivered the work.

We never saw the money and we did not see Barry Smith again either - despite Kevin and myself finding his address in Matlock and trying to confront him.

We lost £4,000 and learned a big lesson.

CHAPTER THIRTY

Growing . . . in many ways

B RIAN O'Connor, whilst retaining a connection with the Palace Group, had forsaken all day-to-day responsibilities and had joined Stewart Jamieson in Security Centres. They had worked very hard to expand the security company to a level which enabled it to become a public company and for shares in it to be traded on the London Stock Exchange.

Following the launch, they set about expanding the company further and diversifying into separate operations. It meant that Brian was spending a lot of time off the Island and undertaking a substantial amount of travelling throughout the UK.

He and Rita, who had moved to Glen Vine from Onchan some years previously, decided that they wanted to have their own property built on the

On one of our early trips to the south of France to stay with the O'Connors near to Grasse. Brian's brother John, a popular priest in Belfast, Gwynneth, Brian, daughter Rita, mother Rita and Brian's Mum.

Our annual trip to St Jacques was an enjoyable affair. On the left, the owners of San Pecaire, the property Brian hired, Monique and Mathieu Bonfonti. When persuaded, Mathieu could be a great storyteller.

outskirts of Douglas - they chose a plot at Hillberry Green. In turn, we were becoming unhappy at York Road - the house was cold and because of its age and construction it was difficult to modernise. Their home at Glen Vine was small but very homely and we liked it so much that we bought it from them when it became vacant.

Brian was determined that he and Rita should have a period of time each year in a warm climate and so he arranged for the hire of a large property, normally for the month of August, in St Jacques, near Grasse, in the south of France. We were delighted to join them for a week during the first year and for every year subsequent until he terminated the arrangement a few years ago. The property had a beautiful pool and extensive grounds - it was a pleasure we looked forward to every year.

The property - an old French chateau-type building - was owned by Mathieu and Monique Bonfonti who made us welcome every year. After some research, we found that in his younger days Mathieu was a member of the French Resistance and, if you got him in the right frame of mind, he could regale you with some excellent stories. They were a lovely couple.

IN 1984 Gwynneth Jr was married at the Royal Chapel of St Johns and we organised a reception for her and her new husband Philip Willson, a member of the Isle of Man Constabulary. Unfortunately, the marriage did not last very long and they were divorced within eighteen months.

By this time, our eldest, Tracey, had begun a career in the civil service and Sarah was at QEII school at Peel.

Steven commenced an apprenticeship at Print Centres in 1983 working under the guidance of Kevin Clarke who had offered to mentor him. I was relieved by Kevin's offer as I felt that it was in Steven's interests for him to be guided by someone other than me. Kevin and I agreed, however, that Steven should, in the fullness of time, be trained in every aspect of the company's operations.

OUR staff had increased substantially in line with the company's expansion and diversification. We were now using good quality, computerised typesetting but we were still sending illustrations to Liverpool for scanning prior to printing. It was costly and at times delayed production.

We calculated that there was sufficient throughput of scanning to justify the installation of scanning equipment of our own and so we made application to the DTI for a grant to assist us in the purchase of the appropriate kit. We knew we had a very good case - we could prove our efforts to bring work to the Island were working and we were not surprised to be advised of the success of our application.

The work we were now undertaking on the production of our own magazines meant that there was a need to separate the magazine origination department, with its journalists' requirement for space, from the general printing origination.

Prince Edward, representing his father's Duke of Edinburgh Award Scheme, visited the Island in the early 1980s. He dined, at his own request, with people of his own age and Tracey was fortunate to be one of those chosen to join his table.

Coupled with the additional space requirement necessary for the new scanner, we needed more room for production and so we took out a lease on a third unit within one hundred yards or so of our printing facility, in the name of Executive Publications.

The Crosfield drum scanner, the first of its kind on the Island, was installed and was very successful from the start - so much so that we began to do scanning work for other Island printers providing them with a quicker service than sending their originals to the UK.

There were problems, however. Cashflow - the lifeblood of any company - was tight and there were times when we spent hours collecting debts to meet our outgoing commitments. The bank lived up to their promise and, when needed which, in fairness was not too often, allowed us to overdraw without any swingeing penalties. We needed more regular income upon which we could depend each month.

ADVERTISING was now producing a lot of revenue for the company. We needed to seperate it from the printing turnover so that when making decisions for the future for each division, we would have accurate numbers from which to make judgements. We decided that the publishing revenue should go into Executive Publications which we had formed as a subsidiary trading operation of Print Centres Limited, and turned it into a separate limited company for the purpose.

It was obvious that *Money Media* was attractive especially to banks and to any operations associated with the finance industry. We made sure that the editorial support and illustrations were as accurate and informative as they could be.

Terry Liddiard was quick to notice the build up of advertising support *Manx Tails* was getting.

"I would like *Manx Tails* to go bi-monthly," he said.

Fortunately we had been expecting this and had actually been prepared for it. We also knew that before too long Terry would be looking for the magazine to be produced each month. We had asked Terry Cringle to take on the editing of *Money Media*. He agreed and this gave me some relief as prior to that I had been doing the job myself. We also appointed Mike Percival as advertising sales representative of Executive Publications. We were making progress.

WE KNEW that the *TT Programme* was a publication with a substantial following and was well supported with advertising. The TT Festival remained the high point for many motor-cycle enthusiasts and they still flocked to the Island annually buying the programme as soon as they arrived.

Investigations revealed that the publication was published by a company in Reading and whilst supporting an event on the Island which was heavily promoted by the Isle of Man Tourist Board, did not in fact, produce any revenue for the Board which they could, in turn, use to offset their spend.

It was reasonably obvious, therefore, that if the programme could be produced in an arrangement which would provide the Board with some income, any proposal along these lines would stand a good chance of success. We put on our thinking caps and contrived a scheme whereby the Board would automatically benefit from a percentage of the revenue gained from the sales of the programme, the advertising revenue would pay for the printing and publishing and we profit from any money which remained.

We met with the representatives of the Tourist Board and argued strongly that whilst the *TT Programme* was too large for any presses on the Island to print, the editorial content, the graphic design, the typesetting and scanning and the publishing of the title should take place on the Isle of Man. We detailed the experience already gained by Executive Publications in the publishing of local titles and our expertise at compiling them. Finally, we put forward our proposal, foremost in which was the suggestion of the percentage of the cover price accruing to the Board.

We knew almost immediately that this was attractive to members of the Board. They had never been offered any income whatsoever from the publication even though it had been produced, purportedly linked with the Board, for many years. It was not a big surprise, therefore, when a few days later we were advised that we had won the contract for three years with an opportunity to renew for a further period of three years upon expiration.

It was, in fact, a good deal for everyone - for the first time, the Tourist Board gained income from the publication which, after all, was published virtually in their name - and we, in turn, would benefit from the publishing profit and would be able to claim more work coming back to the Island as further satisfaction for the Industry Board.

AFTER just a few issues on a bi-monthly basis, Manx Airlines raised the possibility of *Manx Tails* becoming a monthly magazine. We knew Terry was keen for it to happen and, by this time, we were aware of the additional revenue such a move would create and the ease it would provide for our monthly outgoings. It was agreed that the switch would be made at the earliest.

"Manx Tails" became a monthly magazine after a very short time - the new publishing contract was signed by Tim Stevens, Manx Airlines' Marketing Manager, Sue Lord, Executive Publications' Advertising Sales Manager and myself.

We had been joined in the advertising sales department by Sue Lord who took over the departmental management. Sue had worked in publishing previously and she settled in to the work very quickly establishing a good client list in no time.

We had also installed some automated binding equipment in Print Centres which made the finishing of the magazines a lot more efficient and so a switch to monthly, which conformed with *Sea Breezes* and *The Word* schedules, was entirely sensible.

GLEN Vine is a beautiful area and we were very happy there - with the exception of one thing: our family were at an age when they were not able to own their own transport yet had friends in Douglas and needed to spend a lot of time there. This meant that myself and Gwynneth, in particular, became taxi drivers servicing the needs of our family and it wasn't always a convenient arrangement.

Gwynneth was still at Standard Chartered Bank and had now been promoted to Deposits Supervisor. She enjoyed her work there and had developed excellent working relationships with all of the staff at the bank. The drive back to Glen Vine each evening was normally nothing to worry about apart from one incident in the middle of winter when she was caught in a snowstorm and the car slid all over the road. She arrived home unscathed but it was a frightening experience.

We began to search for a property in the Douglas area.

Tromode Park was initially developed by Kelly Bros, the Kirk Michael-based builders. The estate consisted of a number of properties - mostly bungalows - built on the northern side of Tromode Road and the estate was then extended up Slieau Dhoo - the hill behind - with a combination of both houses and bungalows. It remains a very convenient location especially for workers in the town as it is within walking distance and is also handy for the shops and services at Prospect Terrace.

45 Slieau Dhoo was available. It was an "upside-down" house with the entrance, reception areas and kitchen at ground level with all the bedroom accommodation below. It had an excellent large attic and we calculated that with a little bit of alteration to that area it would, at last, enable each member of the family to have their own room.

Glen Vine sold very quickly, probably because it was a lovely area to live and we found ourselves installed in Slieau Dhoo. At the time, our home was the last on the hill, but builders soon became interested in developing the remainder of the estate and within two or three years we had neighbours all around us.

PAUL Gaskell, as part of his promotional activities at the Palace Group, became the promoter of the annual Golf Competition and Gala Dinner organised in the name of Sparks which was, and still is in fact, a well-known charity strongly supported by all participants in show business. It was a fun golf competition played normally on a Sunday afternoon followed by a dinner at which all the show business attendees sat with local people who had supported the event. It invariably produced hilarious results and the majority of the show business guests took a delight in pulling each other's legs.

As we had printed the programme for the event for Paul at a price which reflected the charity aspect of the occasion, he invited me to join in the golf competition which was being held at Peel, my home course. A lot of spectators had turned out to follow the show business personalities around the course and Paul had installed himself as announcer on the first tee informing the crowd, which lined both sides of the first fairway, the identity of the next person to tee off - usually with a facetious remark of some kind. I was the last of my party of four to tee off - the others had all got reasonable drives away and were quite content.

As I stepped onto the tee, "yer man" Gaskell announces, "On the tee, Colin Brown, a member of this golf club and therefore expected to do well!"

Instead of a normal 230-250 yard drive, I think I probably hit the ball thirty or forty yards, no more!

Mr Gaskell thought that this was hilarious and collapsed with laughter and found time to have another go at me whilst I was taking my second shot which, in fairness, was not too far in front of him

I was glad to get away from the first hole and enjoy the remainder of the round.

EUNICE Salmond was the Isle of Man representative for Save the Children and she asked Paul to organise a banquet at the Palace Lido - now a car park - which was to be attended by the Patron of Save the Children, Princess Anne. Eunice was a tireless worker for the charity and later received an MBE for her work, but she was also very demanding and tended at times to expect an awful lot from people.

Paul, as usual, went to town and the tickets sold like wildfire. The after-dinner entertainment was high-class and the Palace Group had done a great job on the menu - it was going to be a great night.

Again, we had printed the souvenir programmes for Eunice and so I was invited, along with Paul and the Managing Director of Manx Airlines, Terry Liddiard, to join the line-up of people who were to be presented to Her Royal Highness.

Princess Anne was introduced to each individual by Eunice and she managed to have a quick word with each before moving on to the next.

She arrived in front of Terry.

At the Save the Children Banquet and Ball at the Palace Lido. Paul Gaskell, left, myself, Terry Liddiard, HRH Princess Anne and Eunice Salmond.

"This is Terry Liddiard, Managing Director of Manx Airlines, the airline which flew you here, ma-am," said Eunice.

"Good evening," said the Princess. "I really enjoyed my flight."

"I'm very pleased to hear that, ma-am," replied Terry.

"And this is Colin Brown - he represents the company who printed the souvenir programme for us," Eunice announced.

"Nice to meet you," the Princess said, "Did you have to gather all the information for the programme?"

"No, ma'am," I said, "Eunice provided some and told me where I could find the remainder."

She moved on to Paul.

"This is Paul Gaskell. He organised the whole event," said Eunice.

"Ah," said Princess Anne, "did you come up with the idea for this?"

"No, ma'am," replied Paul with a very straight face and a nod to Eunice. "We just do as Her Majesty there tells us!"

"Oh, I see . . . just like me," said the Princess with a big laugh.

BRIAN O'Connor's work in Security Centres was flourishing and he was spending a considerable amount of time each week in London. Security Centres had expanded and the flotation had benefitted Stewart Jamieson and anyone else associated with the company.

Brian was keen to repeat the exercise and during an evening out early in 1986 he mentioned that he, in company with local accountant, Tony Thompson, were negotiating with the principals of Island Garages Ltd - the local main Vauxhall dealer - to purchase a substantial stake in the company. Island Garages Ltd was already a public company but its share distribution was restricted to the Isle of Man.

"We have already spent a lot of time with Bob Dowty, who was running things on behalf of the Dowty family - the largest shareholders - and we have come to an agreement on nearly everything," said Brian. "Tony and I want to diversify into different activities so that we can take an enlarged operation to the London Stock Exchange for a public flotation."

"You must be close to an announcement, then," I asked.

"Yes, we are."

"I wish I had some ready cash to invest," I said rather longingly.

"Well, you may not have cash," he responded, "but you do have a successful company."

"Yes, but . . ."

"Print Centres and Executive Publications could be the first of our acquisitions," he said, "our first diversification."

"But motor cars and printing/publishing don't exactly go together."

"No," said Brian, "but they don't have to - the idea of a diversified company is to have interests in as many different activities as possible. And, I promise you, our acquisitions will not cease with Print Centres - we have our eye on a few others already."

"We will pay you the going rate for the company but it will have to be in the form of cash and shares - it would not be possible for us to pay in cash alone."

I was quite surprised at this as, in my naive experience of big business, I had always assumed that, to invest in a public company, you had to buy shares - with cash! The proposal which was being made to us was that we would receive some cash plus shares in the public company if we agreed to allow Print Centres and Executive Publications to become part of the new, diversified operation envisaged by Brian and Tony.

I began to realise that he was very serious and that the whole matter was one which required considerable discussion between Nick, Kevin and myself.

The three of us chewed the matter over on two or three occasions and then decided to invite Brian up to Spring Valley to enlighten us further.

We were all impressed with his openness and the frank manner he described his ambitions for the company.

One of our main concerns was the attention which would be paid to Print Centres after the deal was done and we were part of the public operation. He assured us that the company would continue to be properly and individually operated and that any claims for investment would be considered - he pointed out that it would still be there for us to develop, in other words its future would be our responsibility.

"The whole matter will be carried out professionally," he said, "There will have to be a thorough investigation of your books and a due diligence carried out before we can arrive at a price we would be prepared to pay for the shares each of you hold in Print Centres. But I repeat, our offer will be fair and appropriate to our findings."

He went on to say that he would wish for me to take a seat on the Board of Island Garages Limited, the main board, and that part of my brief as a director would include a responsibility for Print Centres at that level.

There wasn't really an awful lot to discuss after this meeting. Brian had allayed any fears we had on the future of the company, there was no threat to staff and future investment was assured. We would be joining an organisation headed by people we trusted and who we knew had some great aspirations for the development of the new company.

We agreed to become part of Island Garages Limited and, within weeks of the announcement of Brian and Tony's investment and future intentions, on 21st July 1986, Print Centres Limited and Executive Publications Limited became the public company's first acquisitions.

At home, Gwynneth and I looked forward to a a joyful year in 1987 - in the September of that year we were to celebrate 25 years together.

In September 1987 we were due to celebrate our Siver Wedding with a party at Boncompté's, Onchan Head.

CHAPTER THIRTY-ONE

Going Public

THERE were publicity photographs, announcements and interviews to do with the take-over but, apart from that, there was initially little change for Print Centres.

For me, regular meetings of Island Garages Limited confirmed the intentions of Brian and Tony to push on with the expansion of the company. Cowley Groves, the estate agency headed by Patrick Cowley and Terry Groves, became the second acquisition quickly followed by Format - a building and development company headed by Peter Matthews. Tony Thompson's own company, The Associated Trust Company, which he had operated prior to the Island Garages takeover, later joined the "empire".

In no time the enlarged company was now involved in motor retail and repair, printing, publishing, property sales and rentals, building and property development, accountancy and company administration. It was obvious that the name "Island Garages" had become inappropriate - a new name was needed and Cresta Holdings Limited was born.

The target remained - to float as a public company and be quoted on the LSE. Expansion in the Isle of Man, whilst helpful, was insufficient and

acquisitions in the UK came thick and fast: the first being Greenlight Advertising - a London-based agency run by David Brimble and Terry Hudson.

The acquisitions

Brian O'Connor and Tony Thompson embarked on a series of meetings at which their diversification intentions over Cresta were clearly explained.

in graphic design, advertising and publishing were all fascinating. I developed a very good relationship with David Brimble and he opened a branch of Greenlight Advertising in Douglas. David was quite a character - he was an avid follower of the "rock and roll" cult and dressed accordingly which was rather off-putting for some. I recall him attending the launch of the *Isle of Man Examiner's* pink business pages. Naturally, the theme of the evening was "Pink", so David turned up in a pink suit!!

Whilst all this expansion was proceeding apace, Brian and Tony were working hard on the flotation. It was finally achieved in 1987 and I recall a rather riotous dinner party at the Silverburn Lodge, Ballasalla which had been arranged in celebration. Brian and Tony joined the party direct from the London flight after witnessing the launch at the Stock Exchange. Their achievement obtaining a quotation in such a short time was nothing less than remarkable.

1987 WAS quite a memorable year. Twenty-five years had passed in a heart-beat and Gwynneth and I celebrated our Silver Wedding with a party at Boncompte's at Onchan Head where Jamie and Jill, the proprietors, did us proud with a fantastic supper featuring a filét of Manx beef for around 100 guests many of whom had travelled from the UK for the occasion. Brian O'Connor gave one of his unscripted, comical speeches in proposing the toast to us. We then shot off to the USA and enjoyed our first cruise in the Caribbean - the first of many we have enjoyed since.

The previous year we welcomed our first grandchild. Jenny was born in August in Liverpool where Gwynneth Jr had decided to live. As, surely, all grandparents will agree, grandchildren, and especially the first, are always lovely babies and Jenny was no exception.

BY 1988, there were some 25 companies trading as part of the Cresta Holdings Group. Divisional responsibilities were divided into Financial Services, Corporate Services, Construction and Property Services and Care. Print Centres and Executive Publications were part of Corporate Services

along with an advertising agency, a marketing agency, a PR agency, a graphic design agency, other printers and publishers.

Edman Group - a London-based operation run by Keith Fowler, who became a member of the main Board, became part of the continually growing operation. With this acquisition came facilities for specialist print, photoservices and publishing -

Individual photographs of each main board director were taken for the 1988 Annual Report and Accounts.

all London-based. Homefinders Limited, publishers of *Homes Overseas* magazine, became Cresta Publishing turning out *What House?* and *Homes Abroad* as
well. Exhibitions company - Decron Displays Limited - and Eros Mailing, a
promotional distribution operation in Middlesex became part of the
Corporate Services division. In Manchester, PR operation Staniforth Williams
and its subsidiaries were acquired. and the 1988 Report and Accounts revealed
that this division "now served over 250 major clients many of which are
household names". Cresta's turnover for the year, as reported in the accounts
amounted to £41,750,000 - a truly remarkable achievement!

I was greatly interested in everything that was going on especially in
those areas to which I could directly relate.

There was a downside, however. With the exception of David
Brimble who was always very supportive and, to a degree, Keith Fowler, who
was appointed Divisional Director, I found it very disconcerting when Print
Centres became almost a matter of ridicule for our new London "friends" in
graphic design. They viewed the company with a distaste which was almost
visible and although part of the acquisition strategy was to encourage inter-
trading between the various companies, the amount of business which was
sent to Print Centres from London was ludicrously small.

In turn, I could never accept the "value" they placed on their own
work and the exorbitant charges they imposed upon their clients. To me, it
was a scandal that they were allowed to get away with it, but get away they did.
They were also totally profligate and seemed to care little about whose money
they were spending - as long as it was not theirs.

A prime example of this was the appearance on our doorstep at
home just before Christmas of a large box which had been couriered from
London. It was a dozen bottles of claret! The design agency sent the same
parcel to all of their clients - the net cost must have been colossal, but hey,
this was London!

A FEW months after our return from holiday it was all change.

Brian O'Connor had been acting as Chief Executive as well as
Chairman and it was a logical move for the company to move to separate the
two positions. As one would expect, Brian had excellent business connections
in Northern Ireland and when a prominent member of the province's civil
service showed interest in the Chief Executive's role in Cresta, the company
reacted favourably.

John McAllister had risen to the position of Chief Executive of the
IDB - the Industrial Development Board of Northern Ireland. He had carved
a reputation as a determined manager of this element of the province's government and was the sort of executive needed to control all the various
aspects of Cresta. John joined the company and was later followed by Glenn

Thompson who had worked closely with him in the IDB. Glenn took over some Board level responsibilities later, when the Care division was formed.

I was moved from my responsibilities for the day-to-day operations of Print Centres and Executive Publications - handing over those to my brother Nick - to a full-time position with the parent company. My responsibilities at Head Office were to oversee the operations of all of the Island-based companies and to report on them to John and, via him, to the Board.

John McAllister

An Isle of Man-based investment company, Peregrine Limited of which Tom Dootson was a major shareholder along with our old partner Stewart Jamieson, was acquired by Cresta and Tom was invited to join the Board. Tom had vast experience in property development and his knowledge and expertise was most welcome.

We looked to expand the Island-based operations and, with property sales being buoyant throughout the UK at that time, an expansionary move by Cowley Groves looked logical.

With the proximity of Northern Ireland the deciding factor, a search commenced there for viable take-over opportunities for Cowley Groves. Within a few months there were four Cowley Groves Property Shops located in the province - Belfast City, Antrim and Lisburn - and others were in the pipeline. David Creane had taken on the role of manager of the Cowley Groves offices in the Isle of Man and, together, we worked to develop the company's presence in Ireland.

Cresta had also been making further progress in its diversification programme on the Island. Saddle Mews, just off the new Castletown Road at Pulrose, was a innovative idea in the late 1980s - consisting of a group of

Both Nick and myself were assigned new responsibilities in 1988.

small properties built in landscaped gardens and supported by a warden. The properties were made available to people over the age of fifty years and were intended for retirees. The units sold quickly.

On the same site as Saddle Mews, Cresta, through Format, built Saddle Mews Nursing Home and opened the facility as a residential nursing home for the elderly. The home was an immediate success and we began looking for another site for a second home to repeat the exercise. Within months, King's Reach had opened near to Ramsey and Cresta's involvement in nursing homes on the Isle of Man was now substantial and formed the nucleus of the company's later concentration in Care for the Elderly.

ONE of Brian's associates, Tom Forrest, ran another public company - Rockwood Plc. It was fundamentally a logistics operation but Rockwood, too, had followed a similar diversified path as Cresta. One of Rockwood's subsidiary companies was a small printing operation based at Sittingbourne, Kent. It was basically supplying the parent company with all of their stationery requirements which, in itself, were substantial but the company, whilst not in danger of closure, was not making a profit. Tom had appointed his brother Doug as manager with a specific brief to develop the business into an efficient, local printing unit.

Doug, who had good experience in managerial situations, did not have any sort of a printing background and both he and Tom were at a loss to know what was actually required. Through Brian O'Connor, Tom approached me with a request for me to take on a role as consultant to the operation - now known as Rockwood Print - with a requirement to be at the company around four working days a month.

The arrangement meant that I was regularly spending time in Northern Ireland and now in Kent, *Tom Forrest.* in addition to any visits to London in connection with the main Board and my work on the Island. There was quite a lot of travel involved but, for the most part, it was enjoyable.

The visits to Rockwood Print were almost a return to the start-up of Print Centres eight years earlier. Doug was a joy to work with and was quick to pick up and develop a knowledge of the industry. We managed to secure

The membership of the Executive Club Council had changed somewhat by the time this photograph was taken. Tony Thompson, myself, John Fowlds, Mike Henthorn, Mike Pinson, John Allen, Brian Leahy and Eddie Shallcross with the hotel manager and the Club Secretary.

additional business and, as a result of an investigation into the buying arrangements for materials and a comprehensive dumping of useless kit, we started to pull the company round.

PART of Brian O'Connor's brief at the Palace Company where he retained a directorship was to expand business wherever possible. As we all were, he was fully aware of the increase in business which was occuring throughout the Island coupled with the ongoing development of the finance industry. To Brian, it provided an opportunity to create an innovative venture from which the Palace along with other business people would benefit.

He formed The Executive Club.

Twelve of us were circulated with an invitation to join him for lunch at the Palace during which he made a detailed presentation of his idea. The Club would be headquartered at the Palace. It would be properly constituted with a dedicated secretary, its own private room with a bar and staff and would hold regular monthly exclusive forums with visiting speakers. In addition, members of the Club would receive discounts and enhanced treatment at functions at the complex along with dedicated staff to arrange travel and accommodation when members required it - all in return for an annual membership fee.

Those present at the lunch were invited to become the Club's inaugural members and form the Club Council.

The Executive Club was immediately successful and membership rose rapidly. Members appreciated the attention paid to them by Dennis, the Club's popular steward, and the Clubroom itself was an ideal location for members and guests attending dinner dances and functions at the hotel.

The monthly Dinner Forums were very successful. We had representatives from all sections of industry, finance and government as our guests. and, with a limit of eighteen members attending, there was always a rush to secure seats.

WE were all working exceptionally hard and we tried to balance it with some relaxing short breaks.

We all decamped one Friday to Paris where we had booked rooms at the French branch of the St James's Club. It was truly a luxury weekend which fourteen of us, all connected to Cresta, thoroughly enjoyed - some of us

Colin Shaw, who had been a groomsman at our wedding in 1962 returned to the Island for his first visit since he emigrated to New Zealand in 1963. We were delighted to see him again and, in company with as many of his friends as we could muster, had a great time with him. He looked really well and although he had suffered a couple of illnesses, he was in fine form. Gwynneth, Michael and Irene Gilbertson enjoy reminisces with him.

enjoying it too much!! I was told later that on our way home I had severely questioned the check-in clerk at Charles de Gaulle airport as to why she was taking so long to check us in - apparently the poor girl was trying hard to check in the full party and was really doing her very best. I don't recall any of it - I firmly believe it was a fabrication - but it was an excellent weekend.

BACK on the Island, Nick had been making further strides with Print Centres especially in the publishing field.

Terry Liddiard, now with *Manx Tails* publishing monthly, had requested that *Money Media* be separated from the magazine. He wanted to retain the individuality of *Manx Tails* and felt that all of the business news and advertising should not impinge upon the variety and content of the magazine.

He suggested that *Money Media* should continue to be published by Executive Publications entirely independently on a monthly basis and that Manx Airlines would then carry both magazines in their seat pockets.

Printing trade apprenticeships have now largely disappeared but, upon completion of five years training, an apprentice was "banged-out" which involved his colleagues banging the stone in the composing room with anything they could lay their hands on. The apprentice was then given the equivalent of a "tar and feathering" using printing ink and any other liquid, solvent or waste that could be found. Steven, finished his apprenticeship and must have been one of the last in the Island to have been "banged-out".

On paper, this was a very logical and sensible suggestion and one to which Nick immediately agreed. In practice, however, the production of what now amounted to four magazines each month was quite a task. It was one which Nick overcame, however, and before too long *Money Media* became the premier business magazine for the Island - a level at which it has remained ever since.

Nick would readily admit that the main contributing factor in him succeeding was the installation into Print Centres of the Island's first-ever multi-colour press. The Cresta Board fully supported his application and so did the Industry Board. It became an excellent decision all round as the company's turn-around speed and quality both benefitted from the new press.

CHAPTER THIRTY-TWO

Cresta's turn to Care

GWYNNETH Jr had remarried, returned to the Island and was living in Victoria Avenue. Our first grandson, Adam, was born in 1988 and his birth precluded one of our most expensive years as a family.

Weddings are expensive when there is one a year - we had three in one year!!

June saw the marriage of our eldest daughter, Tracey, to her long-time boyfriend Alan Perkin. The wedding ceremony was at St Ninian's Church and the reception was at the Golf Links Hotel with Chef Edward Pepper and Maitre d' Brian Keenan doing sterling work for us and ensuring that, to complement the wonderful weather of the day, we had equally wonderful fare.

Tracey was followed down the aisle by Sarah. Enzo Ciappelli had been part of Sarah's life for many months and they married at St Mary's Church with us returning to the Golf Links for another reception. This wedding was memorable for the attendance by many of Enzo's family who had journeyed from Sicily for the event. It was a good day, partly taken over by a load of high spirited Italians, but with the very best of intentions.

Finally, at Steven's Palace Hotel wedding reception in December after his marriage to Lisa Shawcross, I had to make some comment about the "overdraft we had to take out to pay for the weddings we had funded."

Little did I know that all three marriages were destined for failure leaving the money spent on the receptions something of a waste!

After fifteen years of contented employment at Standard Chartered Bank, Gwynneth was contemplating her future. Despite the experience she had gained and the promotion she had been awarded, deterioration in job satisfaction coupled with a period of annoying illness was very unsettling. Eventually, with my full support, she decided to leave the bank and enjoy a period as a full-time housewife and mother. The Bank, to their credit, decided to mark her retirement with an "in-house" party attended by management and staff and presented her with a number of gifts which were much appreciated.

Gwynneth decided to leave Standard Chartered Bank and the staff organised a lovely party for her on the day she retired.

1989 SAW a steady development of Cresta's investment in nursing homes with properties in Northern Ireland forming the main base but with other operations throughout the UK. Cresta were becoming adept at the operation and it was a logical move for the Board to decide to concentrate their efforts in the field in which they were most suited and which, by now, was producing the most profit.

The first result of the decision was to change the name of the parent company and Cresta Holdings Limited became CrestaCare Limited. Secondly, the company's headquarters were moved from the Isle of Man to Manchester which made access much easier for most of those involved in the Care division.

There were other changes.

As the decision had been made to concentrate the efforts of the holding company in the direction of Care for the Elderly, the main Board became more heavily slanted in that direction and, bit by bit, the other diversified subsidiaries became less important. It was only to be expected but, nonetheless, it was a disappointment to many of us heavily involved in the subsidiary operations.

Rather like fashion, the corporate world comprises of periods during which it is very "fashionable" to have your company involved in certain business practices. The period when diversification was "fashionable" had now passed, consolidation had taken its place and CrestaCare had conformed by moving into a field which itself was very popular at the time.

It soon became apparent that CrestaCare would be prepared to listen to an offer for any of the subsidiary operations - it would make sense as each sale would provide the holding company with working capital which it could plough into its Care division.

Unfortunately, I was fully aware of the amount of investment Cresta had made in Print Centres since the acquisition and knew full well that Nick, Kevin and myself could not afford the figure Cresta would be seeking were we to make advances in that direction. So, for the time being, I had to grin and bear it.

OUR second grandson, Thomas, arrived in March 1990. Gwynneth Jr now had a family of three and her second husband, Chris, was employed by the Department of Tourism.

Lisa, our daughter-in-law, announced that she was expecting for early 1991 and Tracey, our eldest, revealed that she, too, would be giving birth in 1991 - it was going to be a productive year!

At Print Centres, Steven had completed his apprenticeship in 1988 and had proved to be a very big asset to the company. Both Nick and Kevin had ensured that he had a good grounding in every aspect of the industry and he was now providing sales support for Kevin.

CRESTACARE continued to flourish. I was still part of the main Board of the company but I had to admit that much of the business now discussed at Board level was in an area which was alien to me and for the first time I felt superfluous to requirements.

In retrospect, that feeling I had gained was not one which was intentionally forced upon me - my views were always sought and, as far as I know, were taken into account. I was never reluctant to voice an opinion, however, there were certain times when I did not feel sufficiently confident when giving a view on a matter under discussion.

At operations level, David Creane and I were still looking after the Northern Irish agencies although a couple of them had been bought back by the original owners. David and I also had a set-to with one of the managers who was always reluctant to follow the Cresta way of business. It resulted in him suing Cresta and providing both of us with a great degree of concern. John MacAllister was particular supportive throughout and eventually the matter was settled on the steps of the courthouse in Belfast - in Cresta's favour!

A message arrived on my desk at Cresta House that Mr Robin

Mackenzie wished to make an appointment to call on me. I had heard of Robin Mackenzie - I knew he had been Chief Executive of the Royal Bank of Canada, based in the south of the Island which had recently been taken over.

I tried to imagine what on earth he could want?

The subsequent meeting heralded another life-changing moment . . .

In company with our good friends, John and Tricia Allen, we attended a rather sophisticated function at the Nunnery.

August !990, saw Annie Cregeen reach the grand age of 90 years.. We organised a family birthday party for her at Ciappelli's, Noble's Park. Her daughters and son-in-laws flank her at the party.

CHAPTER THIRTY-THREE

Buy-out

ROBIN Mackenzie is not the sort of guy you would miss in a crowd! He is around six feet three inches and built in the manner one would associate with a line-backer in American football.

We chatted for quite a while about business in general on the Island and he gave me a run-down on his career to date including the recent sale of the bank. He had obviously done quite a bit of homework on me and on

Robin Mackenzie

Cresta and was able to surprise me with a couple of bits of information which I didn't realise were public knowledge.

Robin explained his involvement with the Gilbey family and his position as Chief Executive of the family investment company.

"Do you know Walter Gilbey," he asked.

"Not really. I have actually met him and had one brief conversation with him at a social event, but I cannot say I know him well."

The investment company, Mannin Industries, had a number of small interests throughout the Island including a funeral directors in the south of the Island.

"We get our leg pulled quite a bit about that," said Robin. "But it is a good investment. We also are involved with Printagraphics and Castletown Press, and we have an investment in Irvings.

Unfortunately, Les Edwards, the founder of Castletown Press had passed away and I had heard that Mannin Investments had acquired the business and added it to their other investment in

Printagraphics, the typesetting company which had originally been brought to the Island by Fred Wharton and which, on Fred's departure had been taken over by Roy Livermore and a couple of his colleagues..

The conversation changed to Cresta and I explained Cresta's decision to concentrate their development plans in Care for the Elderly.

"How do you feel about that decision?" asked Robin. "You are a main Board member, aren't you?"

"Yes, I was party to the decision," I replied, "and it is the right one in the circumstances - that does not prevent me feeling rather disappointed for those subsidiaries which are now rather less important and could be considered out of favour."

"Why do you not buy back Print Centres then?" asked Robin.

"Frankly, I would love to do so, but it's out of my reach, and out of the reach of us three previous owners - Cresta supported the company with substantial investment during its tenure and the price now required is too high for us."

"Well, in view of that, how would you feel about you, Nick and Kevin pooling your resources along with myself and Mannin Investments in a buy-out of Print Centres?" ventured Robin. "We could then amalgamate Castletown Press, Printagraphics and Print Centres to form one printing operation."

I really liked that idea and began to think positively about the possibities offered by the proposal.

"It would mean that we could offer almost all forms of printing as well as publishing," I said. "My initial reaction would be favourable, Robin, but I would like to think about it and, obviously, talk over the whole proposal with Nick and Kevin."

"By the way," I continued, "is John MacAllister aware of this conversation?"

"He is," confirmed Robin, "I raised the matter with him initially."

"Is he in favour of a sale?"

"He is prepared to listen to offers," said Robin.

I WAS impressed with Robin Mackenzie from the start, in particular with his honesty and the manner with which he approached negotiations. He was not the "pushy" type and despite his relatively wealthy upbringing and private education he was not a person who imposed himself upon people.

Nick, Kevin and myself all knew that the offer would mean that our shares in the proposed new company would be much less than those we enjoyed prior to the Cresta takeover, however, the three companies combined would be worth more overall and so our stakes would have a higher value.

If, on the other hand, we turned down Robin Mackenzie's approach, the alternative would be for an unsettled period of continued ownership by

Cresta and, perhaps, a sale to a company or person who presented a less attractive proposition.

We opted in favour of the approach and Robin began negotiations with John MacAllister to which I could not be party because of my involvement with Cresta.

Within days he brought news that a deal had been struck and we all were allocated our respective ownerships of the new company, according to the level of investment. The new company was to be known as Mannin Printing Limited. Mannin Industries as the main financier held the largest stake, my own shareholding was next, followed by Robin's personal stake and then Nick's and Kevin's.

We began trading as Mannin Printing Limited on 1 November 1990 - 21 years to the day after we began to operate as Print Centres..

Printagraphics were operating out of a unit at Spring Valley Industrial Estate and they moved into the spare space we had available in the Executive Publications unit. Roy Livermore and Tim Crispin had been shareholders in Printagraphics and they, along with Paul Whittaker who had been looking after Castletown Press, formed the senior staffing for that portion of the new company. Some equipment was moved from Castletown, but there was a lot of duplication and some disposals were made. Bit by bit we integrated all the component parts into the new operation and it began to operate as one unit. Executive Publications continued to thrive and advertising revenue was rising steadily.

ROBIN and myself had come to an agreement very early on that we would each stick to our own areas of expertise in the running of the company. He is a skilled accountant and claimed absolutely no knowledge of the printing and publishing industry. In turn I knew very little about finances and we agreed, in view of this, that in the main, we would support each other in decisions affecting our own areas and not become involved in disputes in areas where our individual expertise was insufficient. We continued along these lines for the whole of our working relationship and it worked extremely well.

The new Board consisted of Robin (Chairman), myself (Chief Executive), Nick and Kevin, with Walter Gilbey and Charles Fargher as non-executive directors. I believe that Robin was of the view that as Mannin Industries had Walter Gilbey as a non-executive, Charles could be seen to be representing the three of us and providing balance.

The first few years of the 1990s were not good years for business in the Isle of Man. We began to detect a slow down of trading in late 1991 and it continued into 1992. We tried everything to boost business and were eternally grateful for the buffer provided by the magazines and their revenue. Cash flow became serious and Robin and I had many quiet chats about the future.

We knew that if we didn't do something radical, the company would not see out the year - it was really on a knife edge.

This was where Robin's expertise came into its own. He devised a re-financing of the company - we all had to stump up cash according to our holding - but the re-financing, with the support of the bank, worked and we pulled through the dangerous period.

Probably because of his previous experience as a bank manager, Robin always insisted that we met with the bank at regular intervals and kept them supplied on a regular basis with all of the company's activities and financial performances. His insistence paid off handsomely in this instance as, when the bank realised we were taking steps ourselves to solve our problem, they had no hesitation in contributing to our survival plan. This association with the bank continued for the whole of our partnership and the company benefitted many times from our openness with them.

After the experience we had gained in the early 1980s, cash flow was always a priority for us. Robin was always keen to keep the debtors list at a manageable level and we began to think that it was so important that there was a need for someone to look after the debtors as a specific responsibility working in conjunction with Lesley Edwards, the daughter of the founder of Castletown Press, who looked after all the company's accounts. Originally working for her father, Lesley had stayed as part of Mannin following its formation in 1990.

I had renewed my working relationship with Ian "Flash" Wrigley when he joined the company as a proof reader and we thought that he was an ideal person to take on the responsibilities of debt collection.

Ian took to the role with enthusiasm, made a significant contribution towards ensuring a good cash flow and remains in place to this day.

Following Robin's re-financing, we saw a small recovery in the business. The market was still very competitive but we began to gain new business and things started to look up.

MY ACTIVE participation in sport had moved from football to golf and I had been member of Peel Golf Club for many years, normally playing on Saturday mornings with John Allen, Peter Oates and Alf Kewley. John Sayle, Teddie Kneen, John Moore, and many other staunch supporters of the club also seemed to enjoy their Saturday morning rounds.

In 1991, John, Peter and Alf visited Macroom in Ireland's County Cork to play golf and thoroughly enjoyed the opportunity to sample many of the dozen or so courses within easy reach of the Castle Hotel in Macroom town centre.

After their second visit a year later, I was invited to join the group to make up the fourball.

The visit became an annual event and I haven't missed one trip since

Three of the "Formidable Four" - Alf Kewley, John Allen and Peter Oates take a break in Ireland. Alf Kewley looked forward so much to our annual trips to Ireland with the voyage to Dublin and the subsequent car journey to Macroom a highlight.

that first invitation. The welcome we get at the Castle is always very genuine and, after all this time, we have become firm friends of both management and staff.

We have enjoyed some momentous occasions, one of which happened prior to my joining the party: on the first foray into the Republic three quarters of the party were asleep in the car whilst Alf was driving. On wakening they found their location difficult to find on the map which directed them to Macroom. Instead of driving through Cork, they were in Limerick - in the lousy weather, Alf had missed the turn off to the South!

We found one year that it was a particularly busy day on the golf courses we normally played and were directed to one which was a nine-hole course not too far from Blarney. One of the nine holes was sited so that the player drove his tee shot over a deep valley to a green which was located alongside a cemetary. My drive sliced and headed towards the cemetary. I thought that was it - out of bounds, play another! Suddenly the ball must have hit a gravestone, bounced high in the air and landed on the green. Alf never forgot that day - "The hand of God," he called it!

We played golf in Ireland the day that Princess Diana was buried. We had booked time at Kenmare - a pleasant enough course set in staunch republican country in the south west. As we drove from Macroom, the funeral was on the car radio and when we arrived in the clubhouse at Kenmare it was on their television, watched by around half a dozen of the club members.

We ordered coffee and biscuits prior to playing the round and we noted that the atmosphere was a little tense, particularly displayed by the Steward.

The National Anthem was played on the television. and Alf stood up.

We looked around - his actions were definitely not appreciated by the others in the room! There was muttering and dirty looks.

"What the hell did you do that for," we asked.

"I always stand for the National Anthem," said an unrepentant Alf.

We got out rather quickly and decided that it may be prudent not to venture into the clubhouse for a beer when we finished the round.

Sadly, our great friend Alf passed away in 2011 after a very short illness - we miss him all the time but we will certainly miss his infectious enthusiasm during our stay at the Castle.

NOEL Howarth was a Manx-based publisher of annuals and year books. He had been in business for some time and published, in particular, The *Isle of Man Year Book* and the *Isle of Man Street Directory* as well as a guide to the Island which was circulated on the Steam Packet vessels to all passengers who were using the ferry service to bring their vehicle to the Island - this publication was called *Motoring in Mann*.

The quantity required for *Motoring in Mann* was too large for us to handle at Mannin, but we were involved in the production of the other two main titles he owned.

We were looking to expand our range of publications and Noel had reached a point in his life when he was looking for a regular income.

We did a deal - Noel joined Mannin on the advertising sales and we took over ownership of the two titles.

JAMES, our third grandson and son of Steven and Lisa, duly arrived in January 1991 and Tracey gave birth to Natalie in June of the same year. The Brown family was steadily growing and by the end of 1993 we had another two grandchildren in Grace, Steven and Lisa's daughter, and Luca, who was born to Sarah and Enzo.

By now, Gwynneth and myself were the only residents at Slieau Dhoo, but we still enjoyed the space and the house provided ample room for parties.

When we first moved in, we had arranged for Jim Rooney - who had carried out much of the alterations required when we moved units at Spring Valley - to knock down a wall at the back of the hall and, in conjunction with the small room behind it, build us a bar.

We said for years afterwards that if the house had been the target for a bomb, everything would have been flattened except "Jimmy's Bar" - assuredly, it was built to last!! We enjoyed many good parties around his bar and Jim remains a good friend to this day.

STEVEN took it upon himself to arrange some most enjoyable company golf

Jimmy's Bar at our home in Tromode was the venue for many happy events over the years.

and fishing outings for Mannin Media and we visited Newcastle (County Down) twice, Athlone (County Meath), Dublin - when we stayed at CityWest, on the outskirts, and played the Irish PGA course at Palmerstown adjacent to the famous Ryder Cup venue of the K Club.

One particular incident whilst playing at CityWest ocurred when Robin Mackenzie, my son Steven, my son-in-law Colin Campbell and myself were playing a four-ball and we had added what is known as the "snake" to the normal game. A team of two which loses the hole is said to hold the snake. It is an accruing pot of money which increases in value with each hole lost and is handed over in cash to the winners - those who do not hold the snake - by the losers, when the 18th and last hole has been played..

Steven and I were playing together and had held the snake for a long time when we approached the eighteenth green. As a result there were quite a few euros in the snake pot and more than the total amount staked on the game. After an enormous amount of leg-pulling and raucous comments, Colin and Robin were left with a thirty-inch putt to ensure that they would be paid and not us.

"You had better get this, Campbell," said Robin as Colin stood over the putt, "otherwise it's going to cost us a lot of money!"

Colin was laughing so much at this, coupled with our attempts to put him off, that I swear his knees were shaking.

He managed to gather himself as best he could, but missed!

"Bloody hell," said Robin and stormed off the green in a theatrical manner, accompanied by non-stop laughter from Steven, Colin and myself.

Poor Colin has had to relive that moment on many occasions since and still manages to see the funny side of it!

CHAPTER THIRTY-FOUR

Publishing Development

WALTER Gilbey's contribution at Board meetings was normally confined to a desire to ensure good business practice was applied at all times. We tried hard to comply with this, but there were times when, for example, Walter's regular request for correct diary records to follow up on sales approaches although undoubtedly correct practice, became tiresome. We wished he would contribute a little more specifically along the printing and publishing lines where we definitely needed help.

Our wish was granted, however, when he raised the subject of Dressage - a sport in which he was deeply involved - and British Dressage which was part of the British Horse Society based in Warwickshire. Apparently, British Dressage at that time circulated all their members throughout the country with a quarterly list of events and results. Walter ventured that this could be something around which a new magazine could be based.

We were keen to expand Executive Publications and accepted the fact that, on the Isle of Man, the publishing market was already heavily concentrated and there was little room for more titles. The UK, then, was the only real alternative and so Walter's suggestion was particularly interesting.

Walter introduced us to some of the prominent figures in British Dressage including Desi Dillingham who, at the time, was one of the driving forces behind the sport, and Jane Kidd, a member of the Beaverbrook family and aunt of Jodie Kidd, who was responsible for marketing.

We visited British Dressage's headquarters at Stoneleigh as well as Desi Dillingham's offices in London and Jane Kidd paid a visit to us on the Island.

Our proposal to the organisation would save them a considerable amount of money in postage every quarter and would provide the membership with all the results and forthcoming events on a monthly basis. The result was that we launched *Dressage News* which, in effect was a magazine, containing news and features, wrapped around a centre section of British Dressage information. Jane Kidd became the first editor and we appointed an advertis-

The 10th Anniversary of Manx Tails in 1992 was marked with a reception attended by around one hundred of our clients. Executive Publications' staff includes, from the left - Howard Caine, Mike Dean, Roy Livermore, Kevin Clarke, Joanna Wilson, Felicity Woods, Walter Gilbey, Frances Hampton, myself, Glenda Jones, Noel Howarth, Nick Brown, Sue Lord, Valerie Cottle and Eunice Salmond.

PRINT CENTRES TENTH ANNIVERSARY PARTY 1989

Bindery operatives, Cathy Francere (left), Judy Bennett and May Brown (Nick's wife).

John Allen, with myself and Nick in attendance, proposes a vote of thanks.

Peter Hearsey cuts the anniversary cake in the company of Chief Minister Miles Walker, Industry Minister, Bernie May and the directors.

Peter Hearsey, who was the firm's first customer for colour work, marke the occasion by cutting the anniversary cake.

ing sales representative based in the Suffolk area. There were initial problems by the score in production but, bit by bit, they were overcome.

From our perspective, this was a major step forward as we had secured new business from the UK and had added to our portfolio of titles.

OUR investment in publishing had now grown substantially and I felt that the company name - Mannin Printing Limited - did not adequately portray the activities of the group's operations. We were involved in printing and publishing and had intention to venture into graphic design when the opportunity arose. We were, then, a full-service media group and I felt the name should reflect this. The Board agreed and we changed our name to Mannin Media Group Limited.

ROBIN had got wind of a magazine for sale in the south of England. The offices were based at a marina at Hamble in Hampshire.

The magazine was *Aviation Trader* - a monthly publication covering many aspects of small aircraft operation and maintenance. As the magazine was relatively new, it had not been accepted by the main newsagent chains and the price was proportionately low.

Robin and I rather took to the manager of the operation although we had reservations about the owner who appeared to us to be a bit of a "flash guy". We visited the offices twice and had a number of meetings at which we debated the viability of the magazine and its potential.

Eventually, we half decided to go for it but we thought an independent view on it would not go amiss. We asked Neil Duggan, one of our auditors, if he would take a look at the situation for us - our main concern centred around whether or not the books of the company were genuine. Neil confirmed that everything we had been told could be justified by the accounts and so the decision was now one based entirely upon whether or not the magazine had a future from which we could benefit.

We decided it could and the purchase went ahead. I well recall, on the same day, the three of us standing on the platform of the nearest train station and Robin's comment, "I hope we've done the right thing!"

Unfortunately, we hadn't.

The magazine did not do well and the episode can be recorded as our worst joint decision ever!

WE WERE always on the lookout for good advertising sales representatives - selling space is one of the most difficult sales jobs around as, when you get down to it, there are not too many people just itching to buy a blank space in a magazine. It's not like venturing into a car showroom - you have already made up your mind you are going to replace your old car, the only question is will the cars in this showroom fit the bill. With space sales, the client's need has to be established by the salesman, as most clients do not want to advertise anyway and regard it as an unnecessary waste of money.

It is often said that quality sales people are born with an ability to sell. Their skills may be honed by sales courses, but the basic ability to sell is already in place. The good sales person can quickly identify the unique selling point of the article they are selling and use it to their advantage.

Anne Pacey is a born sales person. Anne

Anne Pacey provided the impetus the advertising sales department needed and later joined the Board of Directors.

worked in the UK in newspaper space sales before she moved to the Isle of Man with her husband Roy. Initially, they ran what used to be known as "Smokey Joe's" café in Port St Mary, but Anne missed sales and she soon found herself on the staff of Isle of Man Newspapers Limited.

After a spell in their advertising sales department, she left to become the Sales Development Manager of local design studio Creative Studios which was run by talented designer Des Clague supported by Steven Quick who previously was Managing Director of Isle of Man Newspapers Limited.

We were searching, as usual, for good sales staff and, out of the blue, Anne applied.

"Come on," she said at the interview, "you know you need me!"

The one thing you could never say about her was she hid her light under a bushel!

Anne was good, though, and she was correct - we did need her.

We already had quite a good sales team which, in fairness, was producing results, but we needed that extra impetus, some new ideas and some additional enthusiasm.

Anne provided all three by the bundle.

Very quickly we saw that she was management material and we asked her to take on the management of the department which she tackled with her usual enthusiasm. The sales staff, in the main, responded to her and she was keen to look to expand the department.

We had heard that the dormant magazine *Manx Life* could be available for purchase and we decided it would complement the other titles we were currently producing.

By this time our editorial department had grown. Valerie Cottle - my friend from years previous when she was known as Valerie Roach - had been part of the company for a number of years. She had edited *Manx Tails* and various other titles for us for some time and she was now supported by Howard Caine. Valerie eyed *Manx Life* with a great deal of enthusiasm and, in company with Anne, proposed that the magazine should be relaunched as an up-market bi-monthly product. The matter was debated at length by the Board some of whom were concerned that the move would narrow the title's appeal. Anne and Valerie won the day, however, and the relaunch went ahead.

We have been very fortunate in that advancing years have provided us with the opportunity to travel and to visit many different areas of the world. Gwynneth and I love cruising and, as this type of holiday has become more available to all, we cruise whenever we can. Some of the memories we have of our cruises and holidays are shown here - clockwise from top left: the lights of Las Vegas - a stop on our way home from a cruise through the Panama Canal; with John and Tricia Allen at Rhodes; enjoying a coffee in Mykonos; with our dinner companions on a cruise in the Caribbean; at the well-known ruins of Ephesus, Turkey.

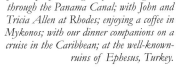

CHAPTER THIRTY-FIVE

The Manx Experience

ONE OF the main customers of Mannin, and before them, Print Centres, was Gordon Kniveton through his publishing operation The Manx Experience.

Gordon was a retired head teacher - his final posting was to Murray's Road School where most of our family had received their primary education. His brother, Ray, was the proprietor of Tours IOM, the coach company who, in the late 1970s/early 1980s, had a contract with certain education authorities in the UK which sent children to the Island for educational holidays.

Gordon found that these children, in many instances, had no literature relating to the Island given to them whilst on the trip and he decided to publish a workbook for them to use whilst they toured about.

I knew Gordon very well and he called to see me with this idea to see if I could offer any advice on the technical side of the book's production. We had a number of meetings and the result was some good business for Print Centres and a new publication called *The Manx Experience* which was essentially a guide to the Island written in a manner readily understood by schoolchildren.

As the years passed Gordon expanded his publishing operations, now called The Manx Experience Limited, by publishing various guide books relating to the Isle of Man such as a guide to the MER, the Steam Railway, *Lady Isabella*, Laxey, Onchan, Baldwin and a number of books about specific areas of Manx life such as *Manx Fairy Tales, Curiosities of the Isle of Man, The Story of the TT,* and many others. In addition, he ventured into publishing Calendars, Christmas Cards, general Greetings Cards and Notelets all with an Isle of Man theme. *The Manx Experience* itself became a general guide to the Island, sought out by many visitors to the Island and was republished every two or three years.

By 1994, he had retired from teaching, was running a relatively large operation by Isle of Man standards and was working rather hard. He suffered

Gordon Kniveton (left) at the Print Centres' 10th Anniversary party with Stewart Watterson and Ken Bawden.

a setback with a slight heart attack and was warned to slow down.

He suggested to me that he would like to dispose of the publishing operations but would like to retain a link with it, especially as a writer.

Gwynneth and I discussed his situation and we decided that between us we could run the venture with me looking after the graphic design, typesetting and origination of the books and the accounts and Gwynneth providing the delivery service to the shops and the link to the retailers.

We did a deal with Gordon, became the owners of a new company which we called Mountside Limited and operated under the trade name of The Manx Experience. Gordon became a consultant to the new company.

Unfortunately, the calendar business faded quite swiftly helped along the way by a decision by Pickwicks - our largest customers for calendars by far - to bring out their own series of calendars in direct competition to us. In addition, the advent of charity cards meant that the greetings card business also failed after a relatively short time.

We decided as a result to concentrate our efforts on the publication of books and produced two volumes of an up-to-date *Chronicle of the 20th Century,* an *Illustrated Encylopedia of the Isle of Man, TT Pioneers, A Century of Manx Transport, Douglas Centenary Album,* along with books by *Peter Kneale, Harvey Briggs, Dusty Miller* and *Robert Kelly,* whose book about Manx cats always sold well.

We managed to do joint publishing ventures with Mercury Asset Management for *TT Pioneers* and the first volume of the *Chronicles,* Barclays for the *Encyclopedia* and one or two other companies assisted in the publication of other titles. It was quickly realised that the books which contained illustrations and text of an historical nature far exceeded sales of any other type of book. A classic example of this was Stuart Slack's work *The Streets of Douglas* which studied the development of the town from the earliest days. Books on rambling, by Peter Hulme and John Kitto also produced a steady sale.

In subsequent years we continued to publish many books - some successful, others not so - to the extent that, when we finally disposed of The Manx Experience in 2008 to Mannin Media, it could boast around sixty titles in its book list.

CHAPTER THIRTY-SIX

Invite to the Mill

JOHN Swale was making noises about selling *Sea Breezes* - he asked us at Mannin Media if we were interested. We were, as the years of experience we had gained through its association with us, had shown us the true value of the title and had brought home to us that it was quite a "cash cow".

John had an aversion to accountants, and wasn't afraid to let them know about it, either. "I don't normally like to deal with accountants, you know. I don't trust them - they are all out to make money out of me. However, you seem a decent enough fella," he conceded to Robin as we sat in his lounge. I expected some tart response, but in fairness to Robin, he took it well and suggested that he hoped John would not come to his normal conclusion about him.

That was the start of a long, drawn-out negotiation during which we had to persuade John that his initial valuation of *Sea Breezes* was much higher than it should have been and that the price we were prepared to pay was more realistic. After many meetings and a number of bottles of whisky, we finally arrived at a price which was acceptable to both parties and Mannin became the new owners of *Sea Breezes*.

Robin and I felt that it would be ideal for Steven Brown to be responsible for the magazine within the group - we saw this as a further extension to his familiarisation with each aspect of the Group. Steven and I spent a week in Liverpool in the offices of *Sea Breezes* where we discussed all aspects of the magazine with the editor and the few staff who remained there looking after the subscriptions and the supplies to wholesalers. We had sorted out the logistics of the operation moving forward and had arranged for the extensive library and filing systems to be shipped over to the Island.

Gwynneth and I then took off on holiday to visit the O'Connors who, at the time, were based in Hong Kong. We were there, on the other side of the world when, in a fax sent to our hotel from Steven, I was advised that Kevin Clarke, along with three members of staff, had served notice that they were leaving Mannin and setting up in business on their own.

I had been aware that Kevin had been unsettled for some time - he had never taken to Robin to the same extent as Nick and myself - but the news of his departure after such a long association was a shock and was enhanced by the three good operatives who also went. However, it was going to happen and there was an upside - our salary bill per month would be substantially reduced!

Because of his access to a lot of company information, Kevin left the company straight away with his colleagues departing at the month end.

KEVIN'S responsibilities within Mannin Media had been print sales and we obviously worried about the effect of his departure on our print sales revenue. Steven had spent a considerable time with Kevin in sales and he was of the view that he could adequately fill the gap. We knew that he would make every effort but we also thought that he would benefit from some additional assistance and experience. At first he required support and advice, but he soon built up a strong client base and was particularly liked by his customers.

At a later date, Steven's department was boosted with the arrival of Lancashire-born, Michael Jordan whose infectious, and at times mad, humour, was a tonic to all - both his colleagues and his customers.

IT WAS really only a matter of time before Anne Pacey joined the Board of the company. She had been attending each Board meeting to report on the revenue levels of the magazines and had continued to be very effective in the running of the advertising department. Her contributions at each meeting were particularly important as Executive Publications had become such an important part of the Group as a whole.

Manx Telecom was an important client of Anne's and they requested her assistance in the organisation of an exhibition which would promote their own products and those of their suppliers and associated businesses. Although it was a little outside her normal remit, Anne took up the challenge and the *Manx Telecom Exhibition* in the Palace Hotel was an extremely successful venture for Manx Telecom and for the Group.

Manx Life was now being produced in the new up-market format and Anne, following the experience she had with the Telecom exhibition, began to think that the magazine could be used as the basis for an annual exhibition. This would be an entirely new venture for the Group, but it would expand the Group's activities further and an exhibition would also fall within the Group's media definition. After great deliberation, we decided to go ahead and Anne began the organisation.

She secured a venue at Summerland which still retained a large hall and a stage which could accommodate Anne's plans for thirty-six stands and special demonstrations and events. The stands and the stand furniture had to be hired from the UK and there was a lot of concern when the weather turned bad, in case the sailings were affected and the stands' erection delayed. In the end all was well.

The event took place in September and, thankfully, the inaugural *Manx Life Exhibition* was a great success with many of the exhibitors commenting upon the good business they had secured.

The event laid the foundation for an Exhibitions Division of the Group in which a substantial investment in stand construction and furniture was made and the *Manx Life Exhibition* became an annual event.

ANNE was also instrumental in the creation of an in-house graphic design studio which we had for a long time wished for as part of the development of the Group. The studio was headed up by Eddie Cassidy who had come to the Island from Middlesborough

The design division grew rapidly, gained a number of high-profile clients and began to supply the printing division with work as a result. The move meant that the Group could now offer a complete design and advertising package to all clients and we began to sell on those lines.

SATURDAY morning, 1997 and I had just completed a round of golf with Peter Oates and John Allen when Peter rather mysteriously said that he wished to speak with me later. Peter had been appointed to the Board of Laxey Glen Mills to work with Henry Robinson in the reorganisation and general development of the Mill following the takeover by the Isle of Man Government in 1989.

In his telephone call, Peter indicated that Henry had decided to retire as Chairman and Peter was to take over his responsibilities. He had been asked to identify someone who, in turn, could be interested in taking his place as a Director and inquired whether I would wish to be that person.

I was flattered. My affection for Laxey remained and I knew the value of the Mill many years earlier when it provided employment for over forty staff. The staff numbers had decreased dramatically but the importance of the Mill in the Island's food chain was undiluted.

My memories of Laxey Glen Mills went back to my childhood when a staff of over forty personnel serviced the grand old building.

I didn't have to think too hard - the opportunity provided me with a totally different industry to study and in which to participate and I accepted Peter's invitation. Peter explained that he would have to propose me to Government which, of course, would have the final say but, a couple of weeks later I attended my first meeting of the Board of Laxey Glen Mills as a new Director.

Driving up towards a place I had known well in my childhood but, frankly, had never thought of since, was a very strange feeling - akin to going back in time. Henry and Peter made me very welcome and I had a good resumé of the part the Mill played in the Island's link between the agricultural aspect of wheat growing and Ramsey Bakery's bread-making. I toured the Mill and met the staff and thought immediately that the place was one of the friendliest I had ever experienced.

Henry duly stood down and Peter and I met once a month, so the job, for me, whilst not exactly onerous, was very enjoyable and offered a welcome change to printing and publishing.

MUM had enjoyed a number of annual holidays with John - they went to Ireland to visit her mother's birthplace and they took a coach tour of Austria, Switzerland and Italy. They also visited the UK regularly and Mum really enjoyed all the trips.

Suddenly, however, we noticed that she had lost interest. Initially, we put it down to her age - she was now 83 - but it soon became obvious that it was something serious She refused to eat and lost weight rapidly as a result.

John became really concerned and after a few consultations with the doctor, she was admitted to Noble's for nursing care. Once there she again refused to eat the hospital food and Gwynneth and May, my sister-in-law, visited daily taking in food, making sure she would eat in in front of them.

After a couple of weeks she had regained some weight and was obviously in better health, but to ensure that she did not stray back to her previous habits we arranged for her to spend a couple of further weeks in Saddle Mews Nursing Home.

Eventually, she returned to Laxey but her original enthusiasm for life had dimmed somewhat and one evening Gwynneth and I were summoned to Noble's where Mum had been admitted with serious breathing problems caused by a failing heart.

She never recovered and we were all with her when she passed away. Mum lived for 84 years and most of them were very happy years, but it could never be said she had an easy life.

IT WAS time to prepare another tender for the publishing of the *TT Programme* for the next three years and, if the Department of Tourism followed their normal pattern, have the contract extended for a further three years afterwards.

Nick and myself with John and Mum shortly before she went into hospital.

We knew that the Department had been most appreciative when we provided them with an income from the publication for the first time in many years. We also knew that our experience in publishing had increased year on year since the programme was published on the Island for the first time six years previously and the programme, in turn, had improved enormously as a result.

Our original proposal to the Department was based upon paying the Department a percentage of the price paid for each copy sold. As the cover price for the programme normally increased each year and the sales remained level, it meant that the Department's income rose year on year. We knew the Department were very pleased with this arrangement - consequently we saw no reason to change it, and submitted our proposal accordingly.

We became concerned when there was a distinct silence from the Department following the meeting at which we understood the matter was to be decided.

We made a few discreet enquiries and found that our proposal had not only been outbid, it had been blown out of the water!

A few months previously, a member of Mannin Group's staff left under something of a cloud and had been provided with employment by Premier Print - Kevin Clarke's new company.

Whilst with Mannin Media he had been privy to all of the information and dealings between Mannin Group and the Department over the *TT Programme* and had, obviously, revealed all to Premier Print. Despite the company's lack of experience in that sort of printing and publishing, Premier submitted an offer, based on exactly the same principle as our own, but containing a cover price percentage to the Department which, in our view, was ludicrously high and specifically aimed to secure the contract.

We tried very hard to recover our losing position and submitted all sorts of additional incentives, none of which, however, came anywhere near the Premier offer. We had to hope that our relationship with the Department and their knowledge of our ability and professionalism would carry us through.

Our hopes were raised by comments from one of the Department members who suggested that we had done enough to save the day, but within days we received a letter informing us that we had been unsuccessful and that the contract had been awarded to "another applicant".

We were rather upset, not so much by Premier Print, but by the Department who, we felt, had completely disregarded the efforts we had made six years hence and the income they had gained as a result of them. In order to avail themselves of a higher income, they overlooked the fact that we had produced excellent issues for six years and awarded the contract to a company which was not able to produce a scrap of evidence of experience in that type of production.

Our confidence in the fairness of Government was severely dented!

BRIAN O'Connor remained with CrestaCare as Chairman for a relatively short period after the deal had been done with Robin and myself over Print Centres. The company became a target for takeover and he departed to become a director of a large business group in Hong Kong. He and Rita were living in one of the many beautiful high-rise apartment complexes in the city with a fantastic view across the bay to Kowloon.

We had not seen one another for a many months and, so we could spend some time together, play some golf and generally catch up, he arranged for Rita and himself to fly from Hong Kong and for the four of us to meet up in the beautiful island of Bali, Indonesia.

Gwynneth and I were quite excited as, apart from visiting them once in Hong Kong, we had not visited any other part of the Far East, in particular, Indonesia, and so it was all new to us.

We flew to Amsterdam and then on to Jakarta, Indonesia, where we had decided to spend a few days befor travelling on to Bali. We enjoyed Jakarta - we had taxi and coach tours and saw a lot of the surrounding countryside. The city itself was interesting as well but we did hear whispers of unrest especially directed towards the immigrant Chinese population. This unrest seemed to increase the day before we left to fly to Bali. The flight was around one hour and we left mid-morning so we arrived at our hotel in Bali early afternoon.

The television was switched on when we gained access to our room. It showed tanks and military personnel surrounding the very hotel we had left

We managed a few good laughs whilst in Indonesia including this signage and a coffee table which was innovative and suggestive, to say the least!

that morning. The uprising had gained momentum and the army had been called in - we were very fortunate in our timing.

We enjoyed a wonderful break in Bali with the O'Connors and it was interesting to note that, at Jakarta on the way home, during the transfer from the internal flight from Bali to our international flight, we were escorted by the army from one airport gate to the next!

THE COMPANY experienced a period when all of the news was bad! Mike Betteridge, our popular computer operator had contracted a terminal illness and we lost John Corkish, a compositor and lovely man, very suddenly to the same dreadful disease.

Steven and myself had been invited to take part in a charity golf event in Castletown and we were just leaving the clubhouse after the round when we took a call from the office with the dreadful news that Roy Livermore had died. He had not been too well for some time and had taken early retirement as a result, but that did nothing to lessen the shock.

THE LOSS of the *TT Programme* was upsetting but apart from that business was good and our financial position was growing steadily stronger. We were approaching the end of the leases we held at Spring Valley and, in the manner many leaseholders regularly do, we started to investigate the possibility of owning our own premises.

The incentives offered by Isle of Man Government were attractive and we visited the Department of Industry to discuss all possibilities with them. A plot of land on the western side of Ballafletcher Road was mentioned by the Department as being available for industrial development - it was part of a block of land owned by the Department intended for that use.

Initially, we thought it not suitable as it was inside the TT course and therefore may present problems during race weeks. The more consideration we gave to it, however, the more attractive it became and eventually we decided to go for it even though the plot size was considerably more than we required.

We applied for planning approval, which was granted without too much of a problem, bought the land and began the building process.

We were devoid of any experience in construction and so we needed to have a site manager to oversee the building. We approached Jeff Magee who agreed to take on the job and arranged weekly meetings with him, normally on site, to discuss progress.

Robin's insistence on retention of costs, coupled with our combined desire to have the building up as quickly as possible, must at times have driven Jeff nuts, but he succeeded and soon, within schedule and within budget, we had fantastic new premises into which we installed replacement, upgraded printing and bindery equipment. We moved in during 2001.

(Top) Breaking ground for the new HQ at Tromode. (Above) The steel structure begins to take shape.

A Mannin Media gathering for retirement presentations to Mike Betteridge (left front) and Roy Livermore (right front). Left to right behind: Barry Costain, myself, Ken Cooil, Paul Whittaker, Cathy Francere, Lesley Woodworth (hidden), Judy Bennett (hidden) Steve Roberts (at rear), Ian Wrigley (hidden), Yvonne O'Hare, Simon Brown, Steve Brown, Marie Cameron, Steven Noon, Peter McElroy Anne Pacey, Jim Rawson (at rear), Sarah Ashall, Eddie Cassidy, Karl Corkish, Philip Richardson, John Corkish, Robin Mackenzie (Chairman), Joe Cannell, Andrew Douglas, Tim Crispin.

CHAPTER THIRTY-SEVEN

A New Beginning

AN unfortunate circumstance in Robin's personal life raised a big issue for him with Mannin Industries and in particular with Walter Gilbey. I took the view that Robin was being treated most unfairly and voiced my views to Walter on two occasions. Nevertheless, Robin was summarily replaced as Chief Executive of Mannin Industries.

Robin submitted a letter of resignation to us which we immediately refused to accept. Supported fully by the Board, I advised Walter that we had full confidence in Robin and that we wished for him to continue as Chairman of Mannin Media Group.

This, of course, was difficult. Walter had taken the view that Robin was not a suitable person to run his operation, however, he remained a member of the Mannin Media Board and if he wished to continue that membership, he would have to be prepared to attend meetings which Robin would chair.

Both Robin and I felt we knew Walter sufficiently well to know that this situation would be too much of a *volte-face* for him. We decided that the only solution was for us to buy out Walter's and Mannin Industries shares in Mannin Media and Robin put his accountancy thinking cap on again.

Within a couple of months the situation had been solved, Robin, Nick, Charles and myself had all increased our stakes in the company and Walter and Mannin Industries were in the past.

BY NOW, Steven was attending every Board meeting and reporting on sales. He had become proficient in all departments of the company and was supporting me strongly in most areas of my own responsibilities.

We invited him to join the Board, which he readily accepted. and Robin and I now were of the view that the Board was properly constructed with him as Chairman and myself as Chief Executive. Nick's specific responsibilities were production and *Sea Breezes*, Anne's were advertising and exhibitions and Steven's were print sales. Charles Fargher continued as a non-executive director.

Our meetings were productive and, in the main, enjoyable. We didn't agree all the time - neither did we spend our time arguing - and the company generally progressed. We decided to invest substantially in Heidelberg printing equipment using six unit presses

Quite suddenly, the Board setup was broken when Anne decided that she needed to retire.

Although we knew she had been under pressure to do so for quite some time, we took the view that Anne would not be able to bring herself to part company with her sales background and we were confident that we would retain her contribution, but we misjudged the situation. Her departure created quite a gap in our managerial arrangements and it was some time before we made proper progress towards adequately replacing her.

We spent some time searching for a replacement for Anne. Robin had been approached by the brother of a South African new resident of the Island who enquired about the possibility of employment for his brother. We felt that it was an approach which needed to be followed up and we invited Terry van Rhyn to visit us at Media House.

Whilst we were certainly satisfied with the qualifications and the references Terry presented, we were still dubious when comparing him with a person we had got to know so well and we questioned how our clients, many of whom were difficult to satisfy, would respond to him. His reactions to our

We decided to apply for accreditation in "Investors in People" and after an extended period of assessment, we were presented with the certificate by Alex Downie, Department of Industry Minister. Left to right: Robin Mackenzie, Steven, myself, Anne Pacey Donald Collings, Minister Downie, Michael Jordan, Liz Corlett and Paul Whittaker. The newly-installed 6-colour Heidelberg is in the background.

many questions, however, were very good and we decided that he should be given the chance to prove himself.

Terry began work with us and immediately impressed. He settled in very swiftly and presented a number of good and innovative ideas especially where marketing our own company was concerned - an area in which we had always been notoriously poor.

Unfortunately, Terry's ambition was to run his own company and within a relatively short space of time, he left to set up an advertising and marketing operation in the town centre.

ANNIE, Gwynneth's Mum, had been living in her own little apartment in Laxey and was quite content. She had reached the grand age of ninety-seven yet was still travelling on the bus to Douglas regularly when she needed to and thought nothing of walking up to the shops in Laxey village when required.

By the age of ninety-nine, her advanced age was beginning to show. She began to forget things and Gwynneth became concerned about her living alone, even though the apartment complex was looked after by a caretaker.

As we had plenty of room at Tromode, we could arrange for a room specifically for Annie and we suggested that she come to live with us again. She moved in and quickly settled in to her new home - it meant that she could see all members of our ever-increasing family almost every day and she was very happy.

Annie celebrated her century in 2000! She received a card from the Queen congratulating her and a visit from the Island's First Minister, Donald

Tricia and John Allen were on hand to help Annie to celebrate her 100th birthday.

Gelling, and his wife Joan - who had been a school colleague of Gwynneth's sister, Anne. She also took delivery of a beautiful bouquet of golden roses from the gardens of Government House, sent with the congratulations of the Lieutenant Governor and his wife.

It was almost as if Annie considered that now she had reached one hundred years old, there was nothing much left to achieve. During the next year her health deteriorated quickly and by August she was bedridden and at a stage where we were unable to adequately cope with her medical condition. Very reluctantly, we arranged for her to enter a nursing home where she could receive the proper care she required.

PETER Oates had decided that he should step down as Chairman of the Mill at Laxey and he indicated that the normal procedure would be for me to take over the chair from him.

Unfortunately, the opportunity arose at a time when I was particularly heavily involved in Mannin Media and I was concerned that I may not be able to afford the time the Chairmanship would entail. Peter and I spent some time discussing the alternatives. I had no wish to divest myself of the connection I now enjoyed with the Mill and, in fact, wanted to become the Chairman, but at a time when I could give the job the attention it deserved.

Compromise!

I approached Bob Briercliffe who had recently retired from a senior post in the Treasury and explained the situation to him. I asked Bob if he would be prepared to stand in as Chairman until I was in a position to take it on - hopefully, in the next two years - and then stay on as a Director.

Bob, who with his wife Pauline, regularly visited Western Australia to spend time with their daughter's family, agreed to the proposal on the basis that the position would be covered whilst he and Pauline were abroad. I was extremely grateful to him.

RELATIVELY speaking, Gwynneth and I had been very fortunate in that we had both avoided serious illness and it was a shock, in late 2001, for Gwynneth to lose her sister at the very early age of sixty years.

Anne had been losing weight for some time and had been diagnosed as having an allergy to wheat - she was being treated accordingly - when she telephoned Gwynneth to request a lift to outpatients as she was concerned about a swelling in her leg.

She was admitted to hospital where the wheat allergy was, after a short time, re-diagnosed as ovarian cancer and very soon afterwards, she passed away.

Gwynneth was in shock - it had all happened so quickly and, as always with such disasters, so unfairly. Anne's husband, Eric, had died seven years earlier and she had never enjoyed the loneliness of widowhood.

IN December 2001, shortly after Anne's death, Gwynneth was paying a routine visit to our doctor when he suddenly raised the subject of her sister's death.

" Have you had a check on your ovaries lately?" he asked her.

"No, not lately," she replied.

"Well I think you should - especially after losing Anne. I'll arrange it,"

Shortly afterwards she attended Noble's, in company with Gwynneth Jr, to have the ultrasound examination. Gwynneth Jr had had some experience of ultrasound scans and remarked upon the length of time it had taken. Gwynneth was advised to contact her doctor the following day for the result.

"They have found something in your kidney, Gwynneth," he said, "and they want you to have a CT scan. I will arrange that as soon as possible."

I was not aware of the problem until she told me at Christmas. We tried hard to get the scan carried out during the following week but the doctor's "as soon as possible" was after Christmas, but she did manage to get it done the first Tuesday in the New Year and we attended the doctor the following day.

"The scan has revealed a tumour in your kidney, Gwynneth," said the doctor. "It does require action as quickly as possible. Do you wish for me to set up for you to see a consultant?"

I'm afraid I answered for her. "No, thank you. We have paid for a subscription to BUPA for many years and I will arrange for it to be done privately."

"That's fine," said the doctor, "and if I can be of any help . . ."

We went straight home and contacted BUPA. We were referred to the BUPA Murrayfield Hospital in the Wirral and two days later we were in the consulting room of Mr Richard Stephenson - a consultant urologist.

Within two weeks of the initial consultation, Gwynneth underwent surgery at Arrowe Park Hospital, a couple of miles down the road from the Murrayfield, and her diseased kidney was removed. She spent two weeks in Arrowe Park during which time I hired an apartment at Hoylake so as to be able to spend every day with her.

Happily, after annual visits over the subsequent five years, Gwynneth got the "all-clear" in 2007.

THE period was an awful one for us both and for Gwynneth in particular. During the week she was about to enter hospital for her operation, we were asked to attend the nursing home as Annie's health had taken a turn for the worse. We were at her bedside when she passed peacefully away.

Within the space of two months Gwynneth had lost a sister and a Mum and had surgery for cancer!

CHAPTER THIRTY-EIGHT

Manx Tails . . . nationwide

MANX Airlines had become part of the British Regional Airlines Group in 1998 and from that date it was only a matter of time until the airline became absorbed into British Airways.

It finally lost its identity in 2002 and we received notice that from that date forward, *Manx Tails* and *Money Media* would no longer be carried on the flights of the new operation.

This presented us with a dilemma.

The two titles now produced a substantial amount of the company's annual turnover - we could not possibly afford to close down the titles without serious repercussions. Continuation of their production did not present a problem - it was how to arrange the distribution of the magazines that was in question. and it was one which we deliberated over for many weeks.

Consideration was given to operating with a "body" of distributors in the same way that the *Isle of Man Courier* had been circulated for a number of years. That possibility was ruled out due to the complaints we knew had been received of copies not being delivered.

Eventually we decided that, although it was an expensive method, a delivery of *Manx Tails* by the postman to each household was secure and, as far as the Island was concerned, was innovative. We also decided that we would revamp *Money Media*, re-format it to A4 and have it delivered by post to all local businesses

Manx Tails is now in its 30th year of unbroken publication - something of a record for magazines in the Isle of Man, and remains as popular as ever.

with additional copies of both magazines to be made available at certain high volume accesses, such as the airport and the sea terminal.

The print runs, and therefore the circulation, of both magazines were increased and the decision proved to be one of the best we made. Both magazines remain in circulation and have gathered enormous respect throughout the Island.

I HAD been a member of Peel Golf Club for more years than I care to remember and had sat on the Club Committee for some five years when I was approached by Peter Dawson, then Club Captain, to stand as Vice-Captain in 2001 and to be Club Captain in 2002.

Alf Kewley was Club President, and I had just persuaded John Allen to put his name forward to join me on the committee. I believed that, in these circumstances and with the members of the committee who would remain in place, by the time my tenure was imminent we would have a very good representation. I agreed, therefore, to Peter's proposal.

Peel Golf Club's constant concern centres around whether or not it can balance the books every year. Inability to do so invariably means an increase in the annual subscription which is greater than inflation and never well received by the membership. A section of the membership, however, demands that the hours that the clubhouse is open for business at the bar - the most costly expense in the club's accounts - remains similar to a public house. Obviously, in order to close the gap between costs and revenue in the clubhouse, it was necessary to either reduce costs, which

Generally, golf club captains are invited, as representatives of their club, to functions organised by other clubs in the area. In this instance I was invited to Ramsey where the club had arranged for a speaker from the Royal & Ancient - the organising body for golfers - to address the dinner guests. He brought with him the Ryder Cup and we each had an opportunity to be photographed with it.

was an extremely difficult task, or increase revenue. It was a fact that a large percentage of the membership did not make any use of the club's bar facilities at all - had they done so, any problem of losses at the bar would have been reduced.

At the time, it was accepted that there was a need for a full-time Manager at the Club. We advertised the vacancy and received an application from Michael Robinson who had spent a considerable amount of his working life employed by the PGA in England. He was able to produce excellent references and, as we were fully aware of his capabilities in organisation, we invited him to accept the position.

One of Michael's first moves was to introduce to the Club a scheme whereby all members paid for their food and drink in the clubhouse using a membership card which would enable them to receive a ten per cent discount on all displayed bar prices. The card acted in a manner similar to a debit card and in order to activate it all members had to place an initial deposit of £50 which was collected with the annual subscriptions. This meant, in effect, that all members, even those who never entered it, paid a minimum of £50 every year at the clubhouse and at the end of the year all accounts, for each member which remained in credit, accrued to the Club. The move immediately reduced bar losses and provided substantial working capital for the Club at the commencement of each financial year.

It is the Captain's responsibility to appoint members of the committee to the various sub-committees of the Club - Greens, House, Finance, etc - and, with a thought to his background in banking, I asked John Allen to chair the Finance Committee.

Towards the end of my tenure, with a view to increasing revenue, we decided to place both Michael Robinson and the very capable Steward at the time, Alan Brew, on contracts of employment which would enable them to earn additional salary directly related to any new revenue they were able to bring to the club. We expected some opposition from them over the proposal but, surprisingly, they were both very supportive and could readily understand the move.

We had a good year and, with the introduction of the card, some small increase in revenue and John Allen's tight control on spending, we had performed much better than the previous year and, after a year which was very demanding but very enjoyable, I handed over the Captaincy with a degree of satisfaction.

Amazingly, within the first six months of the following year, Alan Brew and Michael Robinson's contracts, with the incentive element, had been cancelled and their salaries increased. Not long afterwards, Michael Robinson departed, the £50 deposit on the debit card was reduced to £25 and any credit remaining on members' accounts at the end of the year was repaid to the

At a delightful gathering in the Board Room I was presented with a number of lovely gifts from the staff and from the directors. Left to right, Steven, Robin Mackenzie, Celia Francere and myself cutting the inevitable retirement cake.

members. As a result, all advantages gained through the working capital facility were lost!

Such is life!

I HAD reached the grand old age of sixty-two and I felt that it would be nice to be able to decide to go places without the constraints of daily employment. Steven was proving capable of standing in for me whenever necessary and I raised the prospect of my retirement with Robin.

We agreed that it should be a "semi" retirement with me remaining a member of the Board and taking responsibility for specific assignments as and when they arose. It suited me as I was rather reluctant to divest myself of all connection with the company and wanted to see it continue to develop.

One such assignment was when the contract for the *TT Programme* came up for grabs once again. We were determined at Mannin that we would win back something which we regarded as being rightfully ours. We set about putting together a contract which whilst sufficiently attractive that the Department of Tourism could not fail to decide in our favour, yet still provide the company with good revenue.

The contract was won back.

There was little doubt, however, that the actions of the previous contract holders had made the contract nowhere near as profitable as it was when we initially brought it back to the Island, but it still contributed an annual profit to the company and as the first issue under the new contract was for the *Centenary TT Programme*, we went to town on the production.

ONE other effect of my "semi" retirement was that I was now able to devote time to Laxey Glen Mills and so took over the Chairmanship from Bob Briercliffe who had carried out excellent work whilst standing in for me.

The relationships between the Mill and the wheat growers, on the one hand, and between the Mill and Ramsey Bakery, to whom the Mill sold eighty-five per cent of its product, were always in need of care and attention.

Although we had our ups and downs, Steve Martin, normally the growers' spokesman, Tim Allison, John Corlett and Robert Morrey were regular visitors to the Mill office and invariably we got on well.

There was, however, one rather fraught incident when we agreed to attend a meeting of all growers at the Grosvenor Hotel in Andreas. The growers' representatives and the Mill were deep in discussion over the price the Mill were prepared to pay for wheat from the forthcoming harvest. We had spent a lot of time doing our sums and we had presented the growers with a price which we felt was fair to both sides of the industry. By this time, Mike Henthorn, who had recently stood down as Chairman of the IOM Chamber

Taken as a souvenir of the Mill's 150th Anniversary, the Board of Directors Mike Henthorn and Bob Briercliffe flank the Mill Secretary Fred Newton, with Manager Sandra Donnelly, now Managing Director, and myself.

of Commerce, had joined the Board and he, along with Bob Briercliffe, Mill Manager Sandra Donnelly and myself arrived at the meeting to be asked to wait in the hall to be called in to the meeting.

We commented that it was rather akin to standing outside the headmaster's study!

That comment became even more appropriate when, after eventually being invited in to the meeting, we were, in effect, summarily "bollocked" for having the nerve to offer a price which was unacceptable! We couldn't believe what was said, or the *Jim Duncan.*

manner in which we had been treated. We walked out of the meeting as mad as hell!

Weeks later, after reasoned discussion an agreement was reached which was accepted by all, but the incident rankled in our minds for many months.

James and Caroline Duncan, the proprietors of Ramsey Bakery, became good friends to the extent that James, a very competent baker and confectioner, kindly produced a wonderful cake with which I celebrated my seventieth birthday. I am firmly of the view that the criticism often levelled at Ramsey Bakery about their prices is based more upon envy than fact. Account should always be taken of the fact that the Bakery has a limited market - unlike the Allinson's and the Kingsmill's of this world - and their product is of a much higher quality, less "cotton-wool" and more bread! Jim and Caroline worked hard for many years to ensure the success of the Bakery and are entitled, in my opinion, to all the trappings that success brings.

During my association with the Mill, I came to realise the importance to the Island of the tripartite arrangement of wheat growing, milling and bread making. I became a great supporter of buying local food products whenever possible and will always continue to do so and often rant on about large retailers who, despite their claims to the contrary, are not cost effective to Manx shoppers. The same retailers do not contribute to the Manx economy to the level they should, yet receive the almost grateful support of a Government which is scared stiff of public reaction were they to oppose their desires.

Whilst promoting the Isle of Man at every opportunity, I tend to despair over the "crabbish" attitude often displayed by Manx people. We seem to take great delight in complaining bitterly about local services and the success of local people and then, when they are replaced or deposed, we find we are worse off as a result. It's worth posing the following questions: do we get a better service from Flybe than we had from Manx Airlines? Has the Steam Packet services improved since it was sold to external interests? Shouldn't we be shouting from the rooftops about the success of Mark Cavendish?

I had formed the view shortly after taking over the Chair that the Mill was much too dependent upon the Chairman in its day-to-day operations. I set about raising the status of the manager, Sandra Donnelly. Sandra is a trained micro-biologist with a degree and had been appointed to run the Mill laboratory - a facility necessary to control the standards imposed upon wheat growers by the Mill and to control the quality of flour produced.

When the manager of the day departed the scene, I asked Sandra to take over. At first she was hesitant and concerned about the effect upon staff, growers and customers of having a female running the show. But she stuck to the task and has proved time and time again that she was definitely the right person to handle the job. One of my last jobs as Chairman of the Mill was to propose that Sandra become Managing Director - I'm delighted that she is now in her rightful place.

At the recent 150th Anniversary celebrations of Laxey Glen Mills. Current staff sit on the lorry at the rear, directors in white coats at left front, all accompanied by a large number of staff from previous years.

(Left) Something has obviously amused Steve Martin. (Centre) Director Mike Henthorn presents the poster prize to the young winner. (Right) Manager Sandra Donnelly and director Bob Briercliffe.

CHAPTER THIRTY-NINE

New eras . . .

STEVEN approached me during late summer, 2007. "What would be your reactions if I told you and Robin that I wanted to head up a consortium to buy the company," he asked.

"I imagine that the response would be an expression of interest," I replied. "But how are you going to do it."

"Well, I have raised the matter with a number of people and we have arrived at a consortium of six, including myself," explained Steven.

"If this is a genuine proposal," I ventured, "you will have to take it to Robin - I could not be part of the negotiations due to our relationship, but I would, obviously, be party to the decision should it go ahead.

Steven made his proposal and Robin and I discussed the situation before we raised it with Nick and Charles. Both of us wanted the company to continue its association with the Brown family and this would ensure that progression. Nick was to continue with the company and be part of the consortium,

and Charles was keen to be party to an arrangement which would be of benefit to both Nick and myself.

Negotiations began.

Recognising Steven's admitted inexperience in such matters, Brian O'Connor offered to assist Steven in the buyout and attend any meetings with Robin or the bank where Steven felt his experience would help.

Eventually, after a relatively short series of meetings, a price was agreed and the proceedings of the transfer of ownership began.

It was an odd situation as Steven wanted me to remain as non-executive Chairman of the new company and the matter of bankers to the new owners had to be decided. It was thought that three banks would be offered the opportunity to provide facilities, one of which was the bank which Robin and myself had used for the previous seventeen years.

All three made presentations to the new Board, with me sitting as Chairman. The only bank which definitely did not win favour was the one which had been *in situ*. Their opening suggestion was that the previous owners should have retained a percentage of the shareholding - that went down really well with the new owners around the table and the Chairman!

SO Robin and I bowed out. I had been fifty years in the printing and publishing industry and enjoyed by far the most of it. Robin, despite his numerous claims that he "knew nothing about printing", now knew a hell of a lot about it, and we had formed a close relationship which continues to this day.

I remained associated with the company for a relatively short period but decided that it was not particularly helpful to Steven and his colleagues to have me around too much. Time moves on, and the advances in the industry soon made me realise that my contribution could not create a big benefit. I thanked the new Board for its invitation to remain Chairman, but resigned.

Steven and his colleagues have developed Mannin into a more modern operation with digital graphic design and website creation. The machinery has been modernised much further and can now rightfully lay claim to being one of the most modern on the Isle of Man.

The company has moved forward - Neil Bryden, a qualified accountant, has become an additional investor and he and Steven enjoy much the same relationship as Robin and myself before them.

There are big plans for the future and, with the knowledge of the company's determination, they will succeed.

MY working life ended in 2010 when I stood down as Chairman of Laxey Glen Mills. I had been a Director for thirteen very happy years, seven of which I served as Chairman.

My retirement coincided with the Mills's 150th Anniversary and I was pleased to be associated with a book written and compiled by Andrew Scarffe which detailed the Mill's history.

That year was also a significant year for the Laxey Village Fair as it was the 40th such event since its inception. The Fair is held each year in Laxey Valley Gardens and, in recognition of the Mill's anniversary, I was invited by Steve Rodan, MHK for Garff and Chairman of the Laxey Heritage Trust, to open the Fair.

I had never been keen on public speaking. My throat tends to dry up and I detect a tremor in my voice when I speak, so it was with a degree of trepidation that I accepted Steve's invitation.

After a wonderful reception in Laxey MER station and a parade to the Gardens on a glorious evening I stood to deliver my speech.

Amazingly, I was not nervous at all and I understand that there was no hint of a tremor - I could have gone on for ages!

Maybe it was because of all the memories I have of the area . . . or maybe it was the "presence" of my ancestors located a few yards away at Brown's Cafe!

"There's a great view from this platform . . . Hi!!!"

"My word, I'm enjoying this"!

The invitation to open Laxey Fair was a fitting culmination to my working life. and took place in an area in which, as a teenager, I spent many long and happy hours with my chums . . .

Right: Gwynneth enjoyed it too!

"Yes!!! So glad I came."

CHAPTER FORTY

And now . . .

T HERE is a saying which suggest that life passes by in a heartbeat - as I write this the saying could be very accurate. It seems only yesterday that I sat in Harry Norrey's office in the old *Times* building.

But life goes on and whilst one working life ends another begins.

Retirement is good though . . .

Gwynneth and I have a lovely home now in Birch Hill - a three-bed-roomed property ideal for our own use now the family have flitted the nest. We are free to holiday for as long as we wish and as much as possible, enjoy the warm sun. We are fortunate to have retained all our family in the neigh-bourhood of our home.

Tracey, our eldest, has spent the last 30 years forging a career in the Civil Service and is now a highly respected member of the Probate Division of Government. She leads a contented life with her partner, Chris Hannon, also a civil servant, and her two daughters Natalie, who has just completed a degree course at the Isle of Man Business School, and Lucy, who attends Ashley Hill school, in their bungalow also in Birch Hill.

Gwynneth Jr, although suffering from chronic diabetes doesn't allow it to prevent her enjoying life with her two sons, Adam and Tom in their home in Willaston. Tom has just completed a course at Liverpool training as an elec-tronic music producer. Jenny, Gwynneth's daughter lives a few doors away from her Mum with her husband Aaron and her two children Callum, now a pupil at Willaston, and Abbie - our two great-grandchildren.

Steven married in 2010 in a lovely ceremony and reception in Perth, Scotland. Between running Mannin Media, he lives with his wife Donna and their baby son, Jack at Castletown. James, Steven's elder son, has secured a post at HSBC where he is making excellent progress, and his sister Grace plans to commence a university course later in the year.

Sarah, our youngest, married Colin Campbell in 1999 at Castle Rushen with a reception in Port St Mary. Colin has spent many years in the Island's finance industry and is presently a member of the Isle of Man

Government Treasury team. They live in Ballasalla with Sarah's son, Luca, who finished his final year at Castle Rushen High School in 2012.

At my recent seventieth birthday party, I read out a message which I had received from Malcolm Powell which he had sent to me with my birthday card. I make no apologies for reproducing it here as I believe that it is a very accurate portrayal of those of us who are reaching our advanced years.

WHAT IS A SENIOR CITIZEN?

A Senior Citizen is one who was here before the **"Pill"**, before **"Television"** and before **"Frozen Foods"**, **"Contact Lenses"**, **"Credit Cards"** and . . . before **Man walked on the Moon**.

For Senior Citizens, **"Time Sharing"** meant togetherness not holiday homes, and a **"Chip"** meant a piece of wood. **"Hardware"** meant nuts and bolts, and **"Software"** wasn't even a word.

Senior Citizens got married first, then lived together and they thought **"Cleavage"** was something the butchers did.

To Senior Citizens, a **"Stud"** was something that fastened a collar to a shirt and **"Going all the Way"** meant staying on a double-decker to the bus depot.

They thought **"Fast Food"** was what you ate in Lent; a **"Big Mac"** was an oversize raincoat and **"Crumpet"** was eaten at teatime.

In the Senior Citizens' day, **"Grass"** was mown; **"Pot"** was something you cooked in; **"Coke"** was kept in the coal house and a **"Joint"** was roasted on Sundays.

WE are today's Senior Citizens – a rather hardy bunch when you think how the world has changed!

AND SO the Brown name is continued.

Many years ago, James Brown may have gone to jail for his forthright views on the Isle of Man, but he built a Manx empire with his efforts in the *Isle of Man Times* newspapers. That empire was carried on for many years by his descendants until weeks before my own apprenticeship in the trade began.

It would certainly be fitting for the company my brother and I began in 1979 to continue to prosper and develop under our son Steven in the same manner and enthusiasm displayed by James Brown in the 19th century.

Could it be that the Brown name has something of a continuing role to play in Manx printing and publishing history? May the author be forgiven for hoping so!